ORBS:
The Energy Around Us

SANDY MAYBERRY

BALBOA.PRESS
A DIVISION OF HAY HOUSE

Copyright © 2020 Sandy Mayberry.

All rights reserved. No part of this book may be used or reproduced by any means, graphic, electronic, or mechanical, including photocopying, recording, taping or by any information storage retrieval system without the written permission of the author except in the case of brief quotations embodied in critical articles and reviews.

This book is a work of non-fiction. Unless otherwise noted, the author and the publisher make no explicit guarantees as to the accuracy of the information contained in this book and in some cases, names of people and places have been altered to protect their privacy.

Balboa Press books may be ordered through booksellers or by contacting:

Balboa Press
A Division of Hay House
1663 Liberty Drive
Bloomington, IN 47403
www.balboapress.com
1 (877) 407-4847

Because of the dynamic nature of the Internet, any web addresses or links contained in this book may have changed since publication and may no longer be valid. The views expressed in this work are solely those of the author and do not necessarily reflect the views of the publisher, and the publisher hereby disclaims any responsibility for them.

The author of this book does not dispense medical advice or prescribe the use of any technique as a form of treatment for physical, emotional, or medical problems without the advice of a physician, either directly or indirectly. The intent of the author is only to offer information of a general nature to help you in your quest for emotional and spiritual well-being. In the event you use any of the information in this book for yourself, which is your constitutional right, the author and the publisher assume no responsibility for your actions.

Any people depicted in stock imagery provided by Getty Images are models, and such images are being used for illustrative purposes only. Certain stock imagery © Getty Images.

Print information available on the last page.

ISBN: 978-1-9822-4730-0 (sc)
ISBN: 978-1-9822-4757-7 (hc)
ISBN: 978-1-9822-4731-7 (e)

Library of Congress Control Number: 2020910888

Balboa Press rev. date: 06/18/2020

Dedication

This book is dedicated to my parents, Nick and Georgia, for their love and guidance. I'm thankful to witness their commitment to each other and to serving others.

To my husband, Mike, for loving me, and for his steadfast loyalty and encouragement. He is my rock.

To my daughter, Sarah, who inspires me every day to be a better person; she sets the bar high with her kind ways, her humor and grace, and her respect for others.

To my niece Samantha, for her helpful insights and caring support. You are the epitome of strength, forgiveness, and unconditional love for all people.

To Darlynn, Robert, Sally, Cindy, Amy, Jody, Karen, Kim, Suzan, and Molly; you are the wind beneath my wings.

And to Kristin, for offering her talents to connect the dots and move this project forward, with love and appreciation, I couldn't have done it without you.

—Sandy Mayberry

Contents

Foreword: Sandy and the Orbs ix
Introduction: What Are Orbs? xi
Chapter 1　Surprise! 1
Chapter 2　School Trip 5
Chapter 3　Traveling to Sedona 17
Chapter 4　Meeting Robert 25
Chapter 5　The Search Is On...39
Chapter 6　Meeting Darlynn 47
Chapter 7　The Heart-Shaped Orb at Lake Cypress Springs...59
Chapter 8　September in Newtown, Connecticut, and
　　　　　　October in Oconee, Georgia 81
Chapter 9　Moving Forward 97

Foreword

Sandy and the Orbs

The ability of people to capture orbs with their cell phone cameras and digital cameras is increasingly a special gift of some people. We don't see God or angels, yet we know they exist and are available to us. Now, with modern technology, we *can* see and photograph the unseen. We ask ourselves big questions. What are they? What do they mean? What do they want? Why can some people photograph them and not others? Part of the answer, I believe, is that some people can connect and communicate with orbs.

At important moments in time, orbs appear in photographs and also on video clips in unexpected ways. The photos of orbs taken during the 9/11 terrorist attacks are a perfect example of an awareness beyond our normal senses. We are not alone and not aware of all that is happening within our reality.

When the Kirlian camera was developed in 1939, the energy of the human aura could be photographed, but the equipment was expensive, and the process required more than money, expertise, and opportunity. Now we have all that we need at our fingertips; it seems that only mind and heart are needed now.

This book, with its wonderful photos of orbs, is a perfect gift from Sandy Mayberry. I have known Sandy for several years, and we work together often. She is a dedicated student of the spirit in reality. Her ability to photograph and speak to the orbs she captures on film, I believe, should be attributed to her open mind and, even more, to her open heart.

When Sandy photographed the heart-shaped orb floating over the trampoline in her backyard, it took her to a different level of awareness. This experience was a game-changer for her.

The orbs became more personal and even more meaningful to her at that time. Sandy's investigative nature and ability to find orbs in all types of photos, even old photos from others, is no accident.

As she continues working and developing and receiving new information, she is inviting others to send her their photos. It is interesting to note that so many of these pictures come from the cameras on our cell phones. This means at any moment we can capture a greater awareness of a reality unimagined before this time. I can hardly wait to learn more of the orbs and what they mean to us. Sandy is a gift to me; her work with orbs is a blessing of incredible value. The unseen made visible!

How perfect that we can now expand our awareness in such kind and gentle ways.

Darlynn Bowman, PhD, CMHt, Sedona, Arizona

What Are Orbs?

I'm not sure that anyone really knows what orbs are. Like many subjects, the answer depends on who you ask. Many people have never heard of the term, so they have no earthly idea what I'm writing about. Other people absolutely know what an orb is because they've seen them on photos. Fuzzy splotches, big or little, singular or numerous, invisible in the moment but visible on the photograph, they are considered by some to be camera malfunctions. The word from camera manufacturers is they're specks of dust floating in the air or light reflected in surprising ways. In the psychic community, orbs have long been considered some type of supernatural energy manifesting in our visible world—real evidence of the presence of Spirit.

If you're curious, it might be fun to snap some of your own pictures and see if you capture anything out of the ordinary! Even better, what I commonly tell people who listen to my story is to go home and search through boxes of old, family photos. You may be very surprised, as I was, to recognize something strange and unexplainable on one or several of your photos, photos that you've known existed and that you've looked at for decades.

I have pictures with strange phenomena on them, taken with

my film camera. I had always assumed something went wrong with the film processing. I never gave it a second thought.

Now, of course, some of those smudges are possibly (or definitely) someone's finger in front of the lens, a shadow, or maybe just smudges. But through my education on orbs, their appearance, their movement and color, and also their ability to form shapes other than circles, I believe I can discern what may or may not be the appearance of an orb on a photo.

But I'll get to that later. Prior to June 12, 2013, I had never heard the term *orb*. But I *did* sense that the strange occurrences that I had been seeing on photographs had an explanation beyond the ordinary. I posted a few photos on social media to get started. Most of the Instagram comments I received were along the lines of "What the hell?"

I didn't know how to interpret that comment; I knew it wasn't a question that required an answer. It was more of an exclamation, and although I laughed, I also wanted to yell my response: "I have no idea!" As frustrating as the naysayers were, at least they told me I was on to something. Plenty of other people who contacted me about the orbs believed that they were something wonderful and mysterious, something more than dust, water, or reflections of light. Indeed, they believed the orbs were something, as opposed to nothing. And I was inclined to agree with them.

Finally, a woman from southeast Texas contacted me, and we ended up chatting on the phone for a few more hours than I had anticipated. She and her church community had been photographing and videotaping orbs for several months during their worship services in their sanctuary!

They had come to believe that orbs must be from God, or from angels or spirits. I reviewed the photos on their church website, and they may be right.

I've always had a more scientific approach to the unknown

than a spiritual one, although I would describe myself as a person of faith. I felt the window to my faith crack open a bit more as the woman and I talked about our faith and worship communities. She told me about many things that I wasn't familiar with, such as the occult. I began to consider our conversation a sign that these orbs might be something miraculous.

Though we both agreed that the orbs were something special, neither of us took a stand on what exactly that was. In fact, she kept asking me, "What do you think they are?" I remember saying, "I don't know what they are." I don't know, I don't know, I don't know, came my refrain.

While I was on the phone with this woman, I grabbed a notepad to write down important information from our conversation. The page that I opened to, looking for the next blank page, contained a note that I had made while visiting San Pietro Abbey, in Italy. I wrote down something I had learned there in a story from a Greek writer named Nikos Kazantzakis.

The story was of a man who was terrified of lepers in the time of leprosy. Christ told him that you have to learn to *love that which you fear* and that which you despise—and then have no place for anything but *love* in you. This will rid you of your fear.

I've never felt any fear toward the orbs, although I've had strangers tell me that I should fear this phenomenon. My calm is probably a result of my faith in God, who tells us in our holy scriptures that his presence is always with us, guiding and protecting us, and that we have nothing to fear because we are never alone in this world.

My acceptance of the existence of orbs and my belief that

they are a good energy are different from the views of some other people, and this makes me ponder: How do I see the world? How do I experience life? How do I make peace with the unknown?

My husband later pointed out that the caller's question to me wasn't "What are the orbs?" Her question to me was "What do you *think* they are?" Two distinctly different questions.

1

SURPRISE!

This is a book about mystery, discovery, and awareness. So, sometimes I'll tell you about things that don't at first appear to be about orbs. That's because, at first, they weren't. Not to me, anyway. And then, over time, their meanings revealed themselves. Take, for example, the Sedona T-shirt that just happened to find its way into my closet and that ended up starting me on a path toward understanding...

I had agreed to join friends for a fun-filled day that would stretch into the evening one beautiful but cold-for-Texas day. The day would be bookended by an exercise class and a pizza dinner with friends. Because it was unseasonably cool, I had to dig for a long-sleeved T-shirt in a nearly forgotten box of extra tops stored way up high in my closet. I chose a blue one that my friend Traci had given to me one time when I took care of her house and pets while they were traveling.

Emblazoned on the front were the words "Sedona, AZ. Where good times are had by all." I knew nothing about Sedona, but I knew that this shirt reminded me of a good friend—which is usually what happens with a material object, isn't it? My friend Brandy made me a custom T-shirt for my birthday once that says, "Take Me to the Lake." My family's lake house is my sanctuary. Now that I think about it, I have several friends who are absolutely perfect gift-givers! So, it's not the item itself that we feel a profound connection to, but it's the person who gave us the gift whom we will remember.

At exercise class, we five women set up benches and weights, yoga mats and kettlebells for our sixty minutes together. Diana said, pointing at my shirt, "Sedona supposedly has these vortexes that have energy or something good around them, like the hot springs in Arkansas."

I didn't really know what she meant by most of that, and we didn't have time to discuss as the class started.

Afterward, back home, as the water heated in the shower, I did a quick internet search on Sedona. Quickly, I was sold. I saw beautiful landscapes with tennis courts, hiking trails, and pools all set inside of a beautiful canyon. The entire city and surroundings looked enchanting. It was definitely a place that I should check out, I decided. While I was online, my calendar reminded me that it was the birthday of my dear friend Traci who had given me the shirt from Sedona and started today's little information quest.

My day finally wound down with dinner at one of my favorite pizza places in a development near home called Adriatica. The builder had moved to Texas from a village in Croatia, and he wanted to re-create his country's beauty in north Texas, so all of the buildings are designed with stone and fixtures to look like

Croatia. Even the cobblestone streets and river canals have the feel of a European village. It's very quaint.

When we arrived, my friends didn't want to sit in one of the usual places downstairs, so, encouraged by their exclamations that it'd be so fun to have a drink on the balcony, I followed them upstairs.

We opened the set of double doors at the top of the stairs, and all the people in the room shouted at me, "Surprise!"

And it was! It was a full month before my fiftieth birthday.

Once I settled down from the shock—and thank goodness I'd showered and changed out of that old Sedona tee!—I enjoyed my friends' and neighbors' generous outpouring of love.

It was a beautiful evening after the day's chilly start, and the surprise-party room opened onto the upstairs balcony, so everyone kept stepping outside to look at the sunset. I love the energy at parties, when everyone's reminiscing, mingling, and catching up with each other.

My husband, Mike, and our daughter, Sarah, did a great job of secretly inviting friends, family, and neighbors whom they thought would want to celebrate, and there were some very special, wonderful surprises that night! You never forget people who find a way to make an appearance at specific milestone celebrations. Just as I will always remember every single person who came to visit me when I was hospitalized for a week and diagnosed with type 1 diabetes. I think the saying goes, "True friendship isn't about being there when it's convenient; it's about being there when it's not."

Sandy Mayberry

And though I wouldn't understand it yet, that day offered me more magic: it planted in my mind seeds about Sedona and gave me this photo, which at first I thought was marred but later realized was absolutely perfect...

2

SCHOOL TRIP

Orbs are one of those things that are always with us—have always been with us—even when we are not consciously aware of them. Often, orbs make their presence most known by calling to us from the past. Take a look through your old photos, as I have done mine, and you'll see. Most importantly, those orbs aren't on those photos just to show themselves to you; I believe they are there to offer a much deeper message as well. Consider the orbs I later noticed on photos from a trip of mine that should not have been a great memory…but that now is.

When my daughter was in the fifth grade, I chaperoned her school camping trip. As much as I was looking forward to helping lead the twenty-seven girls in cabin number five, I also was giddy as a camper myself, knowing I'd get to bunk with my three friends Ida, Laura, and Melody, who were my co-chaperones.

We boarded several school buses on a Monday morning in November and drove a few hours southeast of our hometown. The first day was uneventful as we unloaded our duffel bags and camping gear and settled into our cabins, though the day ended spectacularly with entertainment around the campfire. And not surprisingly, it was hard getting anyone to go to sleep even once the girls were bundled in their three rooms of the cabin.

Even we mothers in our room were chatty from under the covers of our bunk beds. Finally, close to midnight, we turned our lights out and tried to rest.

That's when I felt a tickle on my neck.

Pesky mosquitos, I thought, smacking at it. Oh well, I told myself. I needed to suck it up—it was only two nights (and three days, but who was counting).

Ouch!

This time, I definitely felt something crawling on my forearm! Oh, good Lord, my mind was just racing with panic! I am not a camper usually; I'm more of an AC girl.

I took a deep breath and exhaled. *I need to take action*, I thought. *I need to do something, but what? What choice do I have?*

There was a quiet knock on the door. It was Mariah, Ida's daughter, come to escape the girls in her room, who were running around laughing and giggling and not sleeping. As I heard Ida cave and shift over to let Mariah slide in next to her, I felt something tickle my leg. Still trying with every fiber of my being to roll with this situation, I clenched my teeth. A real "go with the flow" move, huh? Yeah, I knew there was no way that I would be able to fall asleep like this. My mind whirled. *I'm going to have no sleep, I'll be super crabby tomorrow, I want to leave now, I can't stand another night of this, why did I sign up for this?* I must have been completely out of my mind!

Oh God, something's crawling in my pajama pants! I realized, just as I heard Mariah say, "Mom, something's crawling on me." That was all I needed to blow the whistle.

I said, "OK, that's it!" I climbed down from the top bunk and scrambled for my flashlight. I found it and ran to the bathroom. I had caught the last one in my pants, and I had to see what it was.

The bug in my hand looked kind of like a brown beetle with wings. I had no idea what it was, but it calmed me to see it. It didn't look too bad. I still had hope that this insect was something harmless. I climbed back into my bunk, but as I did so, I hit the overhead light switch.

I saw bugs coming out of the holes in the wooden frame of the bunk bed half a dozen at a time. "Mother butler!" I shouted in a panic, and maybe I added a few other words.

Holy shit, it was horrifying!

I almost broke my leg jumping down from the ladder. I reached for the light switches and flipped them all on. "Wake up, girls! I've got bugs in my bed!" I pointed the flashlight toward Ida and then Mary and Laura as I said, "And you have them, and you have them too!" Oh, crap, the creatures were everywhere in all four bunks!

The four of us were all on our cell phones searching for "beetle-looking bug that crawls out of your wooden bed frame and bites you when you're sleeping."

Melody said, "Remember, you guys, the teachers and administrators warned us not to have open snacks in our room, or we'd attract bugs!"

I said, "I really don't think it's the chips, girls—the snack is definitely us! We're the food attracting the bugs!"

Sandy Mayberry

We all agreed that we needed help. I texted the nurse, Sandie. At this point, it was 2:00 a.m., and it seemed like the girls in the other rooms of our cabin were unaware that anything was going on.

Normally, I would never send text messages after midnight, but this was an emergency. We all had bugs in our beds, and we were freaking out! And I wasn't really thinking about what time it was.

Nurse Sandie texted back, sleepily, I imagined. She wrote, "I don't know…Can you spray Lysol or something? Do you have anything to spray them with?"

I yelped at the phone as I searched frantically and saw a spray can on the shelf.

"We've got hair spray!"

As I took pictures and videos of the bugs, all of us semi-laughing and making jokes because we were punchy and panicked at the same time, I really thought that we would all have to leave the cabin. I didn't see how any of us would be able to get any sleep at all that night, even though the bugs seemed to be retreating into the holes from where they had come.

Still, we tried. We considered: Can we sleep on the bathroom floor? Oh my gosh, talk about disgusting; that thought was making me sick. Can we sleep in someone's car? Do we tell the girls? Can we sleep with the girls? A million questions and no answers.

Slowly, I said, "The girls might have bugs in their beds too. How do we know?"

We were all looking at each other, trying to figure out if we should wake up all the girls in the cabin and cause mass hysteria or keep this quiet for now and just deal with it in the morning. We chose the latter.

And then Melody said, "If you're wondering what bedbugs look like…"

I heard Laura say, "Oh shit," as I stared wide-eyed at Laura and then Ida and back to Melody. But the description she read from the web wasn't very helpful. Were our bugs oval or rounder? Reddish-brown or browner? And just how long was seven millimeters in length, anyway? On the positive side, this could be something that was completely harmless.

My middle-of-the-night brain had no idea.

"Adult bedbugs appear redder after feeding," Mary said.

On that note, I thought I'd just take a moment to go somewhere and throw up.

Laura chimed in, "OK, I have something from a site called Bedbug Central, *assuming* these are bedbugs. Under the title, 'I Have Bedbugs—Now What?' it says, 'Number one, contact a professional.'"

I said, "OK, we did that—we called for help—so what's next?"

Laura continued, "'The complete elimination of bedbugs requires highly trained and licensed individuals knowledgeable in bedbug biology, behavior, and the proper use of pesticides. There is little chance that you will be able to eliminate the problem on your own. Most commercially available pesticides are not designed for bedbugs, and the use of these products may only spread the bugs to remote areas and make the problem much more difficult to solve. While chemical remedies should only be handled by professionals, there are nonchemical measures you can take to help eliminate the problem and speed up the results of your bedbug program…'"

Waving her index finger in a clockwise motion, Melody said with excitement, "Great, let's speed it up!"

Laura said, "OK, OK, 'remove the bedbugs.'"

We all stood there stunned and looked at each other. We were clueless. She continued, "'Just because you have bedbugs does not mean that you have to wait for a professional to kill them. You can simply crush them with a rag (although this may stain your sheets and pillowcases) or remove them with a vacuum. However, it is important to note that bedbugs can readily infest vacuums.'"

Ida said, "I'm not trying to be negative, but Lysol and hairspray are not professional sprays, and we don't have a vacuum, so what's next?"

"Let's see," Laura said. "It says to eliminate clutter, as it's the bedbug's best friend and pest management professional's worst enemy, blah, blah, blah. Do not store items underneath the bed; don't give them places to hide protected from chemical treatments. Launder items regularly. Heat is deadly to bedbugs, so use hot laundering and a hot dryer over 120 degrees; preferably, up to 150 degrees should be enough to kill a bug infestation."

Melody said, "Shouldn't we just get out of here?"

"No!" Laura said, startling us. "It says we shouldn't change where we sleep!"

I thought, *Oh God, no I can't; nope, no way, I can't do this.*

Laura continued, "This says that if we move to a different area of the home to sleep, the bedbugs will find us."

I'd been able to accept this bizarre night until now, but I suddenly felt like I was in a science-fiction novel. This couldn't be happening, but yet, it was.

We all agreed that there was simply no way that we would be able to sleep in this cabin tomorrow night; we had to get out. We had to think fast.

I closed my eyes because I was so tired and so miserable. I thought about how wonderful it was to not be able to see anything that was directly in front of me. I took my hands and put them over my eyes.

Finally, I sighed and looked again. The room was so bright. "Hey," I said, a realization dawning, "the lights are on." The others were silent. "The lights are on," I said, more emphatically, "and the bugs are gone!" My eyes shifted from each lady.

Together we said, "So, we leave the lights on!"

We all wrapped our heads in scarves and bandanas, whatever we had. Ida had a sleeping mask to cover her eyes; that was a great packing decision on her part. We lay down again, this time leaving all the lights on.

Melody said, "What will we do tomorrow?"

I said, "I'm assigned to the snake building before lunch, and then my afternoon is on the zip line. Laura was assigned to archery in the morning, with rodents and reptiles in the afternoon."

"No, girls, what are we going do about our bug problem? I have no intention of sleeping in here tomorrow night."

I said, "You're right! OK, we have to turn the lights off."

They all screamed at me, "What? No way. No way."

I said we had to do it, because I was going to get a sample to show Nurse Sandie, the teachers, the assistant vice principal, and the lodge administrators.

That was exactly what we did. We turned the lights off and waited.

We didn't have to wait long before the bugs were, once again, coming out to see what they could snack on. Hunting them wasn't that hard.

We knocked a few from our bedframes into tissues, placed the bugs in a plastic baggie, sealed it, and then we were done. We all lay down, leaving all the lights on, and closed our eyes for a couple of hours.

The next morning was strange with sleep-deprived mothers and a cabin full of energetic fifth-grade girls. It felt like we had a big secret, and honestly, we did. The students were all happy, and camp was running as planned, except for us four adults, and Mariah, whom we had sworn to secrecy.

When we stepped outside after breakfast, three of the teachers, Laurel, Kristy, and Courtney, gathered near me to hear about what had happened in our cabin last night.

Laurel looked at me and asked, "What was it like?"

I said, "Oh God, it was disgusting. I remember smacking something that was crawling on my leg, and then my neck itched, so I itched it and smacked that. And then something was crawling on my forearm and then…in my pants! I said, 'Oh no…not in my pants!'" And then I just felt like making a joke, so I said, "'Oh no, don't go there! Well, unless I want you to go there! Unless I give you permission!'"

Laurel laughed loudly, and that provided some comic relief for the moment.

I told the teachers that I had the bugs, so they took the bag and my cell number, so someone could call or text me directly.

Back home at the school, the curiosity and panic were growing among the parents, staff, and administration who hadn't gone on the trip. They had heard from someone that there were bugs reported in one of the chaperone sleeping rooms. But which cabin was it?

My mother will never forget telling the office staff, "Oh, I hope it's not my daughter's."

No one knew at that point how benign or how serious the problem would be. In the end, calming everyone would require an extensive amount of damage control on the part of the school district and the camp owners.

A couple of hours passed, and then I was called to return to *the cabin*.

While I was walking across the campus, I tried to mentally prepare myself for the worst-case scenario. I had already accepted that it was bedbugs. I followed the winding path through the trees and over a couple of tiny bridges. I arrived at the last path that would lead me down to the cabin; I could see our vice principal standing outside the front door.

As I stepped closer, she said, bluntly, "OK, it's bedbugs."

I was prepared for the worst-case scenario, and this was it, so I showed no reaction at all. From what I recall, my face probably appeared as if I'd been shot full of Novocain. But I felt my insides drop, and a quiver ran up through my entire body.

She continued, "We need you, Ida, Melody, and Laura to gather your things and load them on this trailer. We will take everything to the laundry facility and wash it with extreme heat to kill the bugs. And we're moving you and your twenty-seven campers to cabin twenty-two."

I was so tired I said, "You're going to heat everything?" Putting my hands over my chest and searching for some humor, I said, "Are you going to heat us too?"

Kind of a joke, but I was suddenly extremely hot, sweaty, and uncomfortable all on my own. And my brain felt very foggy from lack of sleep, among other things.

As the moms arrived one by one, the exterminator said the bugs may have been in the wooden frames of the beds for a while. The cabin official protested that they treated the cabins periodically for insects and pests. "They're *not* Cabin Ranches bugs!" he cried.

Now that was funny! I said, "Oh, did they tell you where they came from? Because I think they're yours now."

We got through the next day and night in the new cabin. When the camp returned all of our personal items, to four women and twenty-seven girls, most of our clothes were a tight fit. The duffel bags were OK, but caps and hats had shrunk a little, and some of us looked like sausages in our T-shirts and jeans. Kind of a "lumpy look" for me, I'm sure. Ida and I tried to zip up our jeans; neither one of us could zip up all the way. That's what T-shirts are good for—covering up! Even my toes hung off my shrunken flip-flops.

For the ride back to the school, they loaded all the residents of cabin five and our luggage on a bus separate from everyone else.

When we arrived at the school, I'm sure that all of our friends and the staff wanted to hug us for what we'd been through, but I don't recall that anyone did. They waved from afar. Ten feet away, to be exact.

Later, I heard that during that first night the assistant vice principal on the trip had been laughing and making fun of us for texting at such a late hour in our panic.

That's too bad. Now, I can't imagine that if someone were to tell me in advance, "Tonight, you're going to wake up with bedbugs crawling inside your clothes, biting you, and also crawling in your bags," I would not believe them!

Apparently, the administrators and staff on the trip had laughed to themselves: "Yes, you're camping on a school field trip, sleeping in a cabin—there might be a bug! Ha-ha, isn't that funny?"

It wasn't funny at all at the time, but I'm still very proud of us, my cabin-mates and I, for the way that we handled a horrible situation with such humor and grace. And I've grown to love camping now more than ever, with my kids.

I may not have ever paused over the photos from that trip, but the orbs I saw in them during my first review caught my attention—and in turn, my attention continues to shift toward that memory.

We continue to get older, and our children are getting older too. Soon, it will be time to let them go out into the world on their own. That's the best gift that we can give them, the gift of life and their freedom, besides just loving them. I'm so lucky I got to go on that trip, I see with some reflection, and I now reminisce about those days often.

3

Traveling to Sedona

I've always loved the month of June. Not just because it's my birthday month but because it's summer, a break from school and often lighter work schedules, which usually means a family vacation from the daily routine. My endocrinologist told me that I tend to gain weight during the summer, but even that means something good. I respond to my doctor with a wink and an eye roll, "Oh, really? Gee, um…OK." I'm guessing that I like the seasonal fruits; consequently, I eat and drink more during the lazy days of summer. I can't fault my doctors for their observations; they're just trying to keep me healthy. Some of my friends would disagree, but that's great, because that's what friends are for.

The year of my fiftieth birthday, my husband and I and our two kids went to…Sedona! The city that had captured my imagination seemingly quite by accident. We left the Sky Harbor Airport traveling north on I-17, and you can stay on that road almost the whole way. The drive was mostly flat and constant, but the scenery got very dramatic as we approached Sedona.

We turned off the long highway onto State Route 179, a

dazzling display of nature and history framed by towering red rocks. It's no surprise that SR 179 is also known as Red Rock Scenic Byway. We passed the Village of Oak Creek (or Big Park), where the Bell Rock formation rises from the landscape. Bell Rock is known as one of Sedona's most important vortex sites, or a spot where the Earth gives off unique energy.

We were within ten miles of downtown Sedona, and the highway seemed to open up even as the giant red rock formations clustered the horizon. The color was truly spectacular. Blue sky and green pastures, with skyscrapers of rock in layers of burnt orange, gold, and rust, all saturated with mineral deposits and peppered with wildflowers. I'd never seen anything like it. If I had to capture it in one word, I would describe it as *majestic*. What an incredible feeling, slowly driving through the canyons.

We arrived at the gate to our resort, which was made up of dozens of one-story, adobe red rock buildings, reflecting the giants towering around us. We checked in and were assigned an attendant who would show us to our casita. His name was Ty. I've never forgotten him. He was my first clue that many people who worked at this property, and in the surrounding areas, seemed especially happy and healthy.

Ty drove us around the property, pointing out all the buildings and amenities. Near the spa and activities building, he showed us the entrance to the Boynton Canyon Trails and to the vortex.

"There are four or five vortex sites in Sedona," he said. "Each vortex is said to have a different type of energy. The Boynton Canyon Vortex is a site of balanced energy, which means a perfect balance between the masculine and feminine energies on the mesa, or the flat area between the rock formations.

"If you want to go up there," he continued, "use your room key to open the gate right behind the exercise area. It's a private entrance to Vista Trail, which leads to the vortex. I usually walk early in the morning, and it tends to be a little chilly, but the colors of the sunrise hitting the red rocks are quite a sight to see."

Ty pointed toward a tall, skinny tower of rocks that was separated from and in front of the rest of the canyon.

"That formation is known as Kachina Woman," he explained. "If you google it, you can probably find the Hopi Indian legend about her. Though everyone I've talked to around here tells the same story, so whether it's history or myth, and whether you believe it or not, it's an accepted story around here."

Since that first trip, I have returned to Sedona a half-dozen times. Each time, I try to ask numerous people from different backgrounds about legends or myths surrounding Sedona and the nearby Palatka Heritage Site, named with a Hopi word (for Red House) by Smithsonian archaeologist Dr. Jesse Walter Fewkes but not known by that name by the Hopi.

As Ty had told us on our first visit, the Kachina Woman story seemed to be the same no matter who I asked: Hopi, Anglos, and long-time Pink Jeep tour guides. They all said that Kachina Woman towers above Boynton Canyon Land of the Seven Main Canyons. She is a vortex but also a beacon for humankind.

Several thousand years ago, all two-leggeds lived on earth in unity, peace, and understanding. Great Mystery (God) created us in his image and also gave us free will, egos, and a growing, expanding, questioning mind. As our minds expanded with knowledge, our egos and desire to control expanded as well. Some humans began controlling and manipulating others. We created big wars to prove our superiority over others.

Great Mystery was severely disappointed. He moved us from the surface of the earth, with its rich abundance, down to Middle Earth (like the hobbits!), and he gave us a guardian: Kachina Woman. To the Hopi, Kachina was like the Virgin Mary to Christians, Hera to the ancient Greeks, or Lakshmi to Indians.

Kachina was our divine protector, moderator, and overseer. She ruled over us in Middle Earth with a kind, gentle hand but also reported back to Great Mystery often as he rebuilt the planet we almost destroyed.

Several hundred years went by. We behaved ourselves. Kachina went to Great Mystery and told him how well we got along and asked if we could return to the new abundance of the earth's surface, which he had created. He agreed.

Under two conditions. One, Kachina Woman would continue looking after us, looking over us. Two, should we start destroying each other again, Kachina Woman would crumble and fall—as a signal to all humans that Great Mystery was unhappy again, and we would have to straighten up without the guidance or help of Kachina. And that time, he'd move us all to some undisclosed, dark world, never to return to earth's beautiful, abundant surface ever, ever, again.

So, if ever Kachina crumbles or falls, Hopis believe humanity is lost and will soon move to a dark and unknown place worse than Middle Earth.

Ty finished our tour at our red rock building, which was located near the conference center, where many deer frequently roam and nibble on the grass in the early hours of the morning and in late evening. Ty gave us a nice overview of the room and opened the drapes to reveal our balcony. "Oh, see, you have an outdoor grill," he said, "and how nice, you have a view of Kachina from your patio." Also, he said, phone reception was best by the pool, under the watchful eyes of both Kachina and Warrior Man, her male counterpart rock formation.

Ty left us, and we settled in, but we four didn't want to stay in the room long. We all wanted to get to Vista Trail before the sunset. This was exactly the kind of adventure that I loved—walking up the dusty trail lined with crumbling red rocks, winding around green trees and shrubbery, lizards shooting across the trails. There was a yellow "flower tower" growing straight up, very noticeable against the background of greenery. I learned it was the golden-flowered agave century plant. The yellow flowers are framed by blue-gray leaves, and it is hardy to heat, drought, and extremely cold temperatures. There were also strange green plants that looked like vegetation that should be at the bottom of the sea.

Following the trail was a slow incline up the hill and then a short, steeper climb as we approached the legendary rock formation known as Kachina. The word that came to my mind as I gazed up at her was, again, *majestic*. I would guess that many travelers who visit Sedona from all over the world are in awe of the natural beauty and wonder of these canyons.

I took a few family photos on the way up the trail, and then I took four photos of the landscape when we reached the vortex. Standing directly between the Kachina Woman and the Warrior Man, I took a photo looking out upon the vast canyon that would alter my life, and the lives of those around me, forever.

4

MEETING ROBERT

For as long as I can remember, my dreams have often been so vivid that I can recall the people, the places, the colors, the conversations, and all their details for years, even decades. I can still remember dreams that I had when I was a teenager. Sometimes I would dream something about work, and then it would come to fruition a few days later. I asked my friend Sally, who is one of my greatest counselors and mentors, what she thought of dreams and interpretations. She told me that she thought that dreams becoming reality are events of connectivity. For example, when you think of someone and they text or call you, it is because in an unseen way, you are connected.

I remember once, the night before I was to travel home to Indianapolis for Christmas, I felt so sad and lonely. I don't recall why; I was just in a sad place. Suddenly, my phone started ringing. It was my friend Paul, who had never called me; he was my neighbor, and we also played tennis together at the apartment complex. I think you would call him evangelical or charismatic by the way he would talk about his church family. I don't know what it was about him, but Paul really had *the spirit* in him!

I picked up the phone, a little confused, and mumbled to myself, "Who would be calling me now?" It was late in the evening, kind of an odd time to have to answer the phone, so I picked up the receiver, and I said, "Hello?"

The voice on the other end of the phone said, "Hey, it's Paul, I was just thinking of you, and I wanted to wish you a very Merry Christmas, and I hope you have a nice holiday."

I thought, *What inspired him to call me at that moment?* I was stunned. His call was completely out of the blue, or today, people say something like his call was so random. As long as I live, I won't forget the timing of that phone call.

On this morning, I was waking up on my fiftieth birthday. My eyes were closed, and I could still hear the slow, low tones of what sounded like a Native American flute.

Suddenly, I opened my eyes. I could still hear the music, and I could also see the tapestry on the wall over the fireplace in our room. I realized that I was in the hotel room that my family and I had checked into the day before.

I looked at my husband and children; they were all sound asleep. Wow, what a perfect opportunity to find a cup of coffee. I dressed quickly and quietly. As I walked across the parking lot to the path that would take me up the hill to the restaurants, I saw several grayish, large deer grazing in the fields. Of course I stopped in my tracks and quickly backpedaled toward our room so I could grab my camera bag.

There's something very surreal about seeing wild animals

up close. They stop and freeze like statues. Now, I've become so familiar with it, I freeze and play the game of "Who's going to move first?" Deer have a very graceful quality to them.

And the deer that I was seeing this morning were obviously used to the residents watching them, though they remained at a cautious distance. I felt that I took some extraordinary pictures of the beautiful creatures. I was waking up to the fact that I am often a guest in someone else's backyard.

I continued taking photos as I sat with my coffee on the deck of one of the community buildings. As the sun rose in the Arizona sky, I watched the rays of light break through the opening between the Kachina Woman and the Warrior Man rock formations.

It was amazing to watch the color changes on the walls of the canyons as the sunlight hit them. The notebook I used to record my dreams was in my camera bag, so I reached for it to write down a few thoughts about my first morning in Sedona. I wrote:

> I am in such a beautiful place this morning. I was born fifty years ago on this day in 1963 at Our Lady of Perpetual Help in Santa Maria, CA. I've lived on this earth for fifty years, not without trials and tribulations, but I have a good life and I am happy. I feel more content, no, more peaceful than ever on this particular day. The people here are the kindest, most gentle people I have ever met in this world.

At that moment, my mind felt like an empty canvas. I followed what I felt, not what I thought, and I felt like I should walk up the trail and sit on the mesa and quietly make some notes.

As I walked Vista Trail, I read the signs we hadn't noticed the night before. There was general information about preserving the vegetation, such as the century plants (*Agave Americana*) and juniper trees. Signs also listed the insects and animals that I might see while hiking. I took pictures of some large spotted whiptail lizards; most of the lizards that ran across the trail were the greater earless lizards. One sign also read: "Please Do Not Feed the Bears!" I thought, *I am glad I am finally reading these signs!* So many animals make their home in the canyon, including feral hogs. In fact, the first animal I spotted on the trail was a family of furry, grayish hogs. They ran into the woods as soon as they saw me. Sprinting hogs was definitely a sight that I'd never seen before. They run very fast for their stumpy little bodies!

The trail was a soft, red rock, and I was careful not to trip on any fragmented rocks or fallen tree limbs along the way. There are so many interesting sites to look at as you make your way up Vista Trail to the vortex; if you don't pay attention to where you are stepping, this trail can easily become a tripping hazard.

I rounded a turn and said hello to a senior couple who were sitting on some large rocks. I didn't know if they planned to walk up the trail any farther that day, but they were smart for sensing their limits if they chose to go no further. Reminded of my own limits, I took a long drink of water. The altitude, and growing heat of the day, was testing me.

But I wanted to keep going. I felt such a sense of wonder and intrigue at this point—I couldn't wait to get to the mesa. There were tall piles of rocks, cairns, along the way that hikers and trailblazers had created as they walked and prayed and meditated. These stacked mounds of rough stones may be memorials to loved ones or landmarks.

I reached the bottom of the Kachina Woman rock formation. As I looked up at her towering presence, I couldn't help but wonder, *What in the world would make this single tower of rock stand so tall, when the other elements around her eroded away to form the canyon?* I looked at the layers of minerals and the interesting colors of the walls all around the canyon and recalled that I had read Sedona was at the sea floor around 330 million years ago.

Suddenly, I could very clearly hear the high pitch of a flute echoing through the canyon. I decided to follow the music!

There was a man sitting on top of the Warrior Man rock playing his flute.

Every now and then, he would pause to say something about love, trust, or kindness. I didn't write anything down at first, because it was enough just to experience the atmosphere at this point with the few other people who were early-morning hikers. Eventually, I settled in on the side of the canyon, listening to the man play his flute and making some notes about my life so far and my prayers for the future. I wrote:

> Thank you, God, for all of the wonderful parts of my life and also for all of the not so wonderful parts of my life. I have learned my greatest lessons through the trials and tribulations I've experienced

in these first, fifty years. At this point, I am completely open, so I pray that you will use me, Lord, in any way that you can. Whatever you need, I am available—I trust that you will guide me to where I need to be, wherever that may be. Thanks be to God. Amen.

Those questions—Where do I go from here? What's next for me? What shall I do now? —loomed large in my mind. All very common thoughts when you've reached the age of fifty.

The chimes from the flute sounded happy and cheerful, until suddenly they stopped. That was the end of the relaxing music for this morning as I watched this man pack his bag, and then he climbed down from atop the Warrior Man. I couldn't see him very well as he made his way around the base of the rock, but it was taking him a long time to reappear, so I wondered if he was saying hello to each person as he passed them along the way.

He reached the mesa where I was standing, and he was indeed stopping and chatting with the tourists on his way. I didn't dare move; I was way too curious to skip my meet-and-greet with this fellow. I was waiting as patiently as I ever had in my life. I felt like I had all the time in the world to meet this man, and, at that moment, I did.

He finished his chat with a couple, and he walked straight toward me. I put my hands on my heart and asked him, "Are you the man who was playing the flute from on top of the rock?"

He said, "Yes, I was. That was me."

I told him, "Thank you so much for playing such beautiful music. How wonderful, and today is my birthday."

He said, "Oh, my dear," and reached into his pocket. He pulled out a perfectly crafted, burnt-orange, heart-shaped rock and said, "Happy birthday to you!" I was stunned. His gift meant the world to me—it really did. How often is it that a stranger walks up to you and offers you a gift and wants nothing in return? Let me think. Oh…I'm thinking, *never*!

I said, "Oh my, thank you. The first gift I've received today. What's your name?"

He said, "My name is Robert." He continued, "Would you like to know anything about this area? About the place where you are standing at this moment?"

I said, "Oh yes, of course, yes, please tell me!"

Robert said, "This area between Kachina and the Warrior Man is basically in the shape of a figure eight." He motioned with his hand, back and forth, making an *8*, or, as I began to realize, the infinity sign.

Robert continued, "This is sacred ground, and it is the vortex that many people talk about and write about because it is a perfectly balanced area of love between the masculine and feminine energies that are present here."

I was just listening, learning, and taking it all in.

He said, "It's quite an extraordinary place, and the heart I gave you, made from the rock here, to me symbolizes the way that I strive to live on Mother Earth, with kindness and love for one another. That's what I recommend to all people who will listen and accept the gift of the heart."

I said, "Well, you have made my day already, Robert, and I thank you from my heart."

Here I want to pause and connect this story to something that happened the next spring. I attended a writing conference hosted by a book publishing company in Las Vegas. I slipped in late to a break-out session. They had just been discussing signs and symbols. From what I gathered, the specific topic was synchronicity, the simultaneous occurrence of events that have no discernable causal connection but appear significantly related. I heard the speaker and attendees mention that often there are signs helping us see these synchronicities: dragonflies, butterflies, and rocks. Specifically, heart-shaped rocks.

Of course I thought of Robert's gift to me.

And I thought about this for the rest of that day, until finally, by the end of the day, I could think of nothing else. For the final session, the ballroom we were in was still full of people, about eight hundred.

The instructor was wrapping up the session, the day, and the conference. He said, "Well, it's been a great experience this weekend. I hope you all have enjoyed the material, and hopefully, you learned or experienced something good. Does anyone have any more questions before we all head out?"

This was a now-or-never moment for me. The nervous energy is so frightening when you're not used to speaking in public, and not many people are public speakers. But I knew I had to say something because, if I didn't, it would be a missed opportunity, and I was old enough that I didn't want to miss opportunities anymore.

So, I raised my hand and caught the eye of the instructor. He said, "Yes, let's hear from this lady...all the way in the back of the room." I pointed to myself. He said, "Yes, let's get her a microphone." Oh boy, this was my moment.

With the mic in hand, I said, "Yes, hello, everyone, and thank you for such a great seminar. When I entered the room this morning, just before the lunch break, you were talking about signs, and someone asked if a sign could be a heart-shaped rock.

"It happens that the gift of a heart-shaped rock is part of *my* story, and I'm currently trying to write my story. Do you think I should take that as a sign or a connection to this class, or this material, or this conference? It strikes a chord within me, so it feels very special."

The instructor said, "By all means. If you are a person who's paying attention—Oh," he interrupted himself. "We have a woman up here raising her hand. I think we need a microphone up here." The instructor waved and directed the assistant to this woman in the fifth row, close to the front of the room. To the woman, he said, "Yes, do you have something to add?"

The woman said, "Yesterday, my husband and I went up to one of the trails nearby, and we walked for a few hours. I found this heart-shaped rock along the trail, and I considered it to be a blessing, so I have it with me now, and I would like to give it to the woman in the back of the room."

There was a hush in the room, as I suppose many people were moved by this woman's generous offer. I was. How thoughtful that she would want to give me a rock that she believed to be a blessing.

We walked toward each other along the center aisle of the ballroom, with approximately eight hundred people watching, and we met each other in the middle of the room.

"Thank you so much," I said. "That is so nice of you, and this is very special to me." I looked for her name tag and said, "What's your name?"

"Sue," she said.

I heard a gasp from someone in the silent crowd behind me and to the left, in the small section of people who had heard me speak earlier about losing my only sister, my best friend. I heard someone say, "That's her sister!"

Of course, what they meant was that was my sister's name, Sue.

It was an amazing moment, and what a special day at the conference. Sue and I got together, took a picture, and exchanged contact information before we departed from the conference.

What a nice connection. One might ask, what compelled her to want to give that rock away to a stranger? To a person she has never met and would most likely never see again? But to me, it makes perfect sense.

Maybe an angel whispered in her ear, "Sue, why don't you pick a person at the conference, whom you've never met, and give this rock to them. That would be nice!" That was exactly what she did.

And that was exactly what Robert did, there on Vista Trail, on the morning of my fiftieth birthday. Had an angel whispered in his ear too? Either way, we'd felt and acted on a connection. After he said goodbye to me, he continued toward the hikers who were sitting on a steeper cliff at the base of the Kachina Woman.

I sat at the base of Warrior Man for another hour. I gave thanks and prayed. I stacked some rocks and thought about friends and family members whom I'd lost in recent years. I thought about what I had done during my first fifty years of life and made notes about what I might do during the next chapter that was about to begin. This place appears to be a crazy and disconnected world, but actually, we are more connected now than at any time in our recent history.

I am committed to making an effort to find something good in every situation and person. Even if sometimes the good is *really* hard to find. I wrote in my notebook:

> I want to live a life that's meaningful. I want to live an intentional life where my goal is to give back to and to serve others. I want to be purposeful with my words and actions.

Some lofty goals, indeed. As I began to climb down the steps of the canyon to walk back on the trail below, some bugs were buzzing at my ears.

I reached into my backpack and pulled out a set of ear buds. I could no longer hear the noise of the bugs buzzing around my head when I played music.

I listened to Donna Summer, whom I had worked with on performances for corporate shows, and I thought about what an incredible life I'd led. I felt an overwhelming sense of peace. Not indifference but a sense of contentment in knowing that I would walk back down the canyon soon and see my family. And I didn't think that they would be worried about me at all. This was already a fabulous day for me, so, as far as I was concerned, it would only get better. And it did.

In the early evening, we went to a restaurant in town for dinner. It was a warm and inviting Italian place where the lighting and ambiance were perfect for a celebratory dinner. The menu said that the executive chef of the restaurant had a book for sale, and I thought that a copy would make a nice souvenir. The manager brought a copy of her book to our table and then said that the executive chef and author, Lisa, routinely stopped in at each of her restaurants to say hello to her patrons. She told us that she would send her to our table when she stopped there.

It wasn't long before Lisa approached our table and sat down with us. She was very welcoming and kind and well-spoken. She told us about her Italian heritage and how she had a growing desire to see all the regions of Italy and also how much she had always had a love for cooking. She had moved to Sedona from the San Francisco Bay Area, and that added to the conversation because I have a favorite aunt in Sausalito whom I like to visit when I'm working in San Francisco. When I do so, I rent a bike and ride it over the Golden Gate Bridge. I spend the day with my relative and take the ferry back to the city.

After our lovely meal, I got up to walk around and peruse the photographs and décor in the restaurant. There were many pieces of art and paintings on the walls. I noticed an area that seemed to be dedicated to a young adult male.

There was a candle burning underneath the painting of him, which was hanging on the wall near the kitchen's entrance. I sensed an immediate connection to this young man for some reason. I was not yet aware of his story, but I knew he and I had something unique in common.

The next day, back at the hotel, I sat by the pool and read Lisa's book. As I flipped through the pages, I noticed she had a section dedicated to her son. It was a brief tribute to his life and accomplishments with some beautiful pictures of his nineteen years on this earth.

It also explained the years that she struggled with heartache after the day he borrowed her bicycle to ride across the Golden Gate Bridge. He never came back. Investigators searched and exhausted every lead they had for the first year of her life without him and never returned any solid evidence regarding his disappearance. Lisa took a trip to Sedona to try to help heal and ended up deciding to move there.

I was having such a great time exploring the beautiful red rock canyons and talking with the friendly people that I could feel the magnetic pull to stay there and live there peacefully. In fact, on the first morning, which was my birthday, when I sat along the ledge of the rock formations and gazed across the canyon, I said to myself, "I can stay right here, forever." I felt the sense of overwhelming peace and calm wash over me.

On the last morning of our vacation, I suggested we drive to Oak Creek Canyon, which was closer to Flagstaff, before we packed everything and drove to the airport. We debated whether we had enough time to go on an excursion that day, but that Sunday was a very special day. Another day to celebrate, as it was Father's Day!

What a wonderful day to take daughters to a beautiful

national park. This area surrounded by mountains, desert, and ponderosa pine forests is a gateway to the San Francisco Peaks, home to Arizona's tallest mountain, Humphreys Peak.

I only knew the name San Francisco as a city in California, and there in Arizona, the San Francisco Peaks are a mountain range over twelve thousand feet high. Surrounded by pine forests, this lofty area feels like a slice of the Rocky Mountains has been chopped off and transplanted into the middle of Arizona. I was stunned not only by the beauty of this place but by its connection to everything, and the photos I took on that Sunday would corroborate that.

5

THE SEARCH IS ON

Back home in Texas, I was curious about a circle of light I could see on one of my photos from Sedona, and that curiosity, for some reason, would not go away. What did it matter if I had some strange-looking circle on my photo? Did anyone even care? Would anyone care? Or was it just me and my ego? Still, I wanted to know more about it.

You can't connect the dots moving forward; you can only connect them looking backward. So, I had to trust that my relentless curiosity was leading me somewhere. My search for answers became a state of mind that was inspiring me to share my story with others, and in return, I was discovering the connections I have with other people's stories.

Looking back, this was the beginning of the *journey of my life*, and it would last for many more years than I could imagine. I had no idea what I was signing up for. All the while, I could have just let it go. But one thing I have learned on this journey is that doing *something* really is better than doing *nothing*.

Doing something gets us out there, it makes us connect and

discover other people, and it makes us feel alive. At the least, it makes me feel that I'm in a life of discovery, and that makes me feel good. Some people would say it raises my vibrational level, and that is good.

Back to the beginning of the search.

Let's see, I thought, *practically anything I'm looking for I should be able to find online. I will certainly find some type of explanation for this, and then I can forget all about it and go on with my life. I can go back to my routine.* I should say, my routinely boring life.

I searched for "Bubble on my photo." This produced lots of advertisements for soaps, liquids, and cleansers.

I also learned about a place in Waco, Texas, that manufactures "bubble homes." They are very cute and affordable adobe manufactured homes.

Cute but clearly not what I was looking for.

I made some real-world investigations too. Some ended up being humorous. My friend Karen sent me four photos from her hairdresser that he had taken of his family. White, yellow, and orange circles floated around his family members. She asked for my opinion of the photos.

I reviewed them and said, "Karen, I've never seen anything like this. The colored circles of light on these photos don't look like any I've seen on pictures that I've taken."

I was stumped. That left us both curious. When Karen went to have her hair done next, she asked her stylist about the photos. He said, "Oh yes, there's an app on my phone that allows you to put an effect on your photos. It's just for fun, just a little creative effect."

Oh well, at least I'm good at making fun of my earnestness and moving right along—nothing more to see here, folks!

Fortunately, many of my explorations were serious. Friends and relatives were actively watching for anything out of the ordinary that they saw on photos, and then they were sending me the photos to review. I was getting photos from all kinds of people from all around the US.

It was fun to make those connections and see the excitement it gave people to watch for circles of light on their photos, and it was also a challenge for me to review and comment on them.

There are absolutely spirit orbs and phenomena on photos from some of my very close friends and neighbors, but there are also many times that the colored circles of light are reflections from the camera or something else shiny nearby. I began hoping I'd take another marked photo, and finally, I did, though tragically, it happened during a time of great family pain.

My husband's brother, Steve, had just turned fifty. His and his wife, Suzan, had raised two sons in Texas, but they were both in college now. So, Steve and Sue decided it was a great time for a new adventure: Steve would accept a promotion at work, and he and Sue would relocate to Virginia.

What none of us could have foreseen was Steve's diagnosis of a very rare and aggressive form of colon cancer that same year. He was treated at Johns Hopkins in Baltimore, and then he and Suzan moved back to Texas and set up hospice care at my mother-in-law's home in Carrollton, Texas, where they had all grown up.

Steve began having dreams about Granddaddy Bowman, Mama Mayberry, Buster, and Mitchell, his father. They appeared on a green hillside. Steve told them how good they all looked to him, and then Buster did a cartwheel for him, saying that they felt pretty good too! In one visit, his father told him, "Soon." This saddened us greatly, but it also made us feel much more relaxed about Steve crossing over. Steve was the biggest skeptic about things like this, but the dreams during his last days of rest seemed to open his mind.

The day after the "soon" dream, I was playing tennis with my friends Donna, Kris, and Lisa. I got this overwhelming feeling that I needed to drive to Carrollton and see Steve, and I needed to go immediately.

It was just after 11:00 a.m. Over the phone, I said, "Steve, I can't wait to see you." He simply said, "And I can't wait to see you."

I arrived at just past noon in my sweaty tennis clothes and cap. No matter, he didn't care. I was blessed to say a few words to him before he closed his eyes and began to drift into unconsciousness. Friends and relatives came in and out of the house to visit all afternoon.

My husband, Mike, arrived around four o'clock, and after an hour or so, we went to a local restaurant to pick up some food to bring back to the house for dinner.

Steve passed away at 8:10 that evening. It was a Tuesday in late March, so his funeral services were on Good Friday, two days before Easter Sunday. The children brought some orange balloons to the grave, so they could have a little "release ceremony."

I took a few photos of the balloons, and when I saw these photos sometime later, I noticed that Travis and Kyle, Steve and

Suzan's sons, had circles of light on their jackets, and a giant ring floated above Travis's head as he watched the balloons float up to the sky. When I took a closer look at the photo, I noticed six more circles of light in blue and white on his jacket and on his friend, Elisabeth, who was standing next to him. Travis and Elisabeth got married in Jamaica three years later, and they are very happy together.

So now I had two photos whose markings I could not deny. I had been present when they were taken; I had even taken them. I knew they weren't just dust, dew, or reflections of light from the sun.

But I couldn't go back to the internet, and I honestly couldn't think of one person who would know anything about this.

After some time had passed, I had a wild idea. I called the hotel we'd stayed at in Sedona and spoke with Kathy at concierge services.

I said, "This is just a shot in the dark, but I stayed at your property last year, and while I was there, I photographed something curious when I was walking the trails in Boynton Canyon. I'm looking for someone, really, anyone, who might be able to offer some guidance with this type of phenomena. Do you have any thoughts?"

Kathy responded, "Well, I'm not sure what you're looking for, but I can tell you who helped my daughter. Not too many years ago, she had some challenges—she was looking for some *guidance*, as you say—and a lady named Darlynn Bowman, here in town, really helped her to get back on track, and she's married now. She has a good career as a nurse. And I'm a grandma! I'm happy to say that my daughter is doing very well."

I said, "That is wonderful news, thank you, and I'm so happy for your daughter and her family. Do you think I could contact Darlynn for help? What is her job, exactly?" Was she some magical counselor/historian/tour guide, to be able to help both this woman's daughter and me?

"Darlynn seems to be so many things. Some refer to her as a medium, some sort of healer. She's definitely been a guidance counselor and a spiritual doula. I'm not so sure about that one, but it sounds good! So, to answer your question, I'm not quite sure if this is what you're looking for, but you should give her a call, and then if you come back to visit with her, you definitely should stay here and visit with me!"

What a great idea, to return to Sedona, and to do so accompanied by my dear sister-in-law, Suzan, who had just lost the love of her life. For her, this was a time for grieving, a time for reflection, and a great time to be with loved ones who would lift her up and distract her from her sadness.

I called Darlynn that day and filled her in. "I'm looking for some help with a few curious photos that I've taken recently."

Darlynn said, "Oh yes, of course. Well, let's get an appointment, and you and your sister-in-law can come over and visit."

Sue and I traveled on Mother's Day. The first week of May was a lovely time to travel, quite a treat for us, and our kids didn't have to wait on us that day, so I hope that was a break for them too!

Suzan and I met a few times for lunch and shopping prior to our trip to discuss what we wanted to see and do while we were in Arizona. She bought special boots where you turn a handle that makes metal spikes pop out from the sole. She was ready to hike the dusty red rock trails of Sedona! She also ordered some clothes and other travel gadgets to take with her, as she was very excited to be going on a trip to experience a new landscape.

Our trip was a little over a year after her husband had passed away. Time can go so slowly when your partner has passed from this world and your children are grown up and on their own, and it's just you and maybe a dog or cat. In Suzan's case, two furry cats named Clyde and Hyde, who keep her entertained and her spirit joyful.

Sudden loss never seems fair to the ones who are left behind.

Sandy Mayberry

Every day can be a struggle when you miss your loved ones, but day by day, things can get better.

I think Suzan and I both felt we'd gain what we needed in Sedona.

6

MEETING DARLYNN

> We create our lives on a daily, almost a minute to minute basis with every decision we make, so what you think about is what you create. You have a stake in your future.
>
> Darlynn Bowman

The resort in Sedona left us a beautiful little dreamcatcher tile in our room as a welcome gift. I love the saying by Marcel Proust that's engraved on the back of it:

The real voyage of discovery consists not in seeking new landscapes but in having new eyes.

Taking that to heart, Suzan and I decided to hike the trails before dinner. We took a stroll to the concierge desk in the main building, and lo and behold, we got to meet Kathy! It wasn't something I had expected because I knew she worked during the day, and it was getting toward the evening.

She took one look at me and noticed the T-shirt that I was wearing. It was emblazoned with "Santa Maria, California." Just a novelty shirt that I'd received as a gift for my birthday. Kathy said, "Sandy, are you from Santa Maria?"

I told her, "I was born there, but we moved to Wisconsin when I was three years old. It is a special place to me, just because my family lived there, and it's where I came into the world. I traveled there as a young adult with my parents to reminisce, and I think it is beautiful the way the city sits in the valley."

Kathy said in a very curious way, "My daughter lives in Santa Maria."

We were both a little stunned. That moment when you think, *Well, isn't that a strange coincidence.* Some people call these moments, *God winks.*

I was a little stunned but maybe not surprised to have yet another connection with Kathy, Sedona, and all the other little messages that seemed to be revealing themselves along this journey of discovery.

We asked Kathy if Robert was on the rocks, so to speak. Robert is a treasure, offering his hand-carved rocks to any visitor who is willing to accept his gift and doing so never when you expect it but just when you need it. I wanted Suzan to meet him as soon as possible.

Kathy said, "He doesn't work for us, so we never know when he'll be up there hiking the trails and playing his flute, but many days he hikes in the morning and then again at sunset, so you have a good chance of seeing him if you're hiking up the trail now. I'm leaving for the day, but I will look forward to seeing you tomorrow!"

Fortunately for us, Robert was up on the mesa playing his flute that first night. Between phrases of song, he talked about vibrations and seeing the unseen. Everything in the universe is made up of energy vibrating at different frequencies. Even things that look solid are made up of vibrational energy fields at the quantum level. This includes you. All vibrations operate at high and low frequencies, within us and around us.

Robert has touched thousands of travelers with his gift of the heart-shaped rock and his kindness and generosity. What he was saying certainly sounded logical to me, and his delivery was so matter-of-fact. I felt like I was beginning to wake up; I was experiencing new territory.

I felt like my journey of discovery was beginning.

I asked Robert when he came to greet Suzan and me that night if any of the hikers he met on the trail ever refused to accept a heart-shaped rock.

He said, "Oh yes, many people who visit don't speak English, so they don't understand and think that I may be trying to sell them something, so they just wave me away. But I certainly have more people who accept the rocks than people who refuse them."

Suzan said to me, "Let's ask him if we can take a picture with him." I thought that sounded like a great idea, so we took a photo with Robert, and I took a few more photos on the vista.

I asked Robert if it would be OK if I were to write a blog or story about our experiences in Boynton Canyon and publish our pictures. I'm sure I'm not the first person who's been moved by the beauty of the landscapes and the pleasure of meeting and getting to know Robert!

He said, "Absolutely. Write about anything you want and use any pictures you want. We need as many messengers to deliver the message of universal love and kindness. Our world is so lacking right now of people who share good stories. So much doom and gloom. You bet—do whatever you can to keep the positive vibrations flowing."

How nice it was to have his blessing and also have a picture with him as a keepsake. I didn't see any orbs on the pictures I took that time, but what great memories I have of meeting and spending time with Robert, who is welcoming to all.

That night, as we drove past the canyons at sunset to go to dinner, I was so happy the scenery was putting on its usual spectacular show for my sister-in-law. The sky was layered red, blue, pink, and orange, the way children sometimes pour layers of colored sand into a jar. We were going to a very special place in town, where the chef opens the doors to his restaurant promptly at 5:00 p.m. Patrons arrive at 4:00 p.m. to stand in line and wait to be seated at one of his tables. I wondered about that, but we decided to join in, and believe it or not, the wait is worth it. A true, farm-to-table restaurant, where the chef creates his dishes each day based on what he grows in the garden and can purchase at the market each morning. The evening was such a treat, dining and watching the sunset over the canyons of Sedona.

Suzan and I got up early the next morning to more brilliant color as the sunrise burst through the canyons. We were excited to meet Darlynn. All we knew was what the hotel concierge, Kathy, had told us about her experience with her daughter and that for many years, Darlynn taught a class in ethics at the nearby college. She also had a lot of experience in counseling and volunteering, especially with wounded-veteran charities. From my brief conversation with her on the phone, my impression was that we would be meeting a very interesting and intelligent lady and that she was a very humorous person, as well.

We drove through town on Highway 89A, passing all the quaint shops and restaurants until we got to a residential part of town. We found Pinon Drive and turned left under its trees. Suzan and I saw people walking their dogs and others playing with their children and grandchildren, and we stopped at a lovely pink home with a polar bear on the mailbox and a banner at the front door that had four letters displayed vertically: *H O P E*. That was it. We had found our destination!

We parked our rental car in her rocky, circular driveway. We grabbed our notebooks and stepped out of the car. There Darlynn stood, looking through her screen door. What a darling lady—with strawberry-red hair and the sweetest smile, she welcomed us into her home. I felt like I knew her already, even though I'd never met her.

Her home was very comfortable and inviting. She offered us each a bottle of water and instructed us to please have a seat. She had a comfy couch where you could put your feet up. Darlynn sat in her favorite chair where she had pillows to support her back and a walker in case she needed help standing up or sitting down.

We filled out short informational sheets, which Darlynn said she'd refer to as we talked, to help her track our stories. When I suggested Suzan should go first, she told Darlynn all about meeting and marrying Steve and raising two boys and, finally, his unexpected death. Suzan presented herself as a woman on a mission. Truly a woman who was ready to fight tooth and nail for a cause, and the cause was colon cancer.

I remember her saying, "I'm determined to make my mark on the world. I want to leave on this world something I've done, so people can remember me."

Finding herself at a crossroads, widowed at the age of forty-eight, she must have ached for a new direction and a new perspective—she had half a life left, as far as she knew.

Darlynn carefully thought about what Suzan had told her. I could see her digesting the information and choosing her words very carefully. What would she say? What advice would she have to give to her?

She said, "Yes, I see." She hummed to herself and said, "As for the fundraising campaign, I think that's good. It's a good cause, one that will give you a sense of purpose. I understand that the cook-off event that you created and organized raised a lot of money and awareness for colon cancer. That is a very noble task, indeed…" She paused as if searching for the right words and then continued, "I just think you should also make your own personal health and happiness a priority.

"What I'm saying is you should enjoy your time here. You deserve that. You cared for your husband, for your parents, and for your sons, and you've earned your time. There are so many problems in the world, I just hate to see you put so much energy into stamping out cancer. Many people do this, and some of them end up pretty stressed out, and they damage their own health trying to help. What I'm recommending is a balance in your life. Again, I commend you for your spirit, but you should make your own health a priority."

We three women continued chatting and laughing. I was right that Darlynn had a good sense of humor. She has a great laugh and the sweetest smile.

Finally, I said, "Darlynn, may I ask for your opinion about something I have here on my iPad? It's a photo that I took in Boynton Canyon."

It didn't take her long to respond once she saw the photo. "Oh yes, that's a spirit."

I was stunned at her very quick answer.

I was at first speechless, but I also wanted to laugh. Hearing that voiced aloud made it sound…preposterous! "A spirit?" I finally just repeated.

Sandy Mayberry

She said, "Yes, oh yes, when I lived in Pensacola, Florida, there were many orbs on photographs. The sky appeared to be just covered with them. You should google it. Look for the pictures, pictures of orbs—they're on the internet."

Her delivery was very matter-of-fact, yet I was still trying to accept the whole *spirit* thing. If the bubble was a spirit, who was it? Did I know the person or the people? Was the bubble a ball of energy?

Was this just random, or did it have anything to do with me? I was guessing that it did not. It was some kind of strange area that I had stumbled upon, and it was just a fluke that an unidentifiable circle of light flashed onto one of my photos.

So many questions and not too many answers, but Darlynn was helpful.

I showed her the rock from Robert that I had been using as a paperweight at the pool but that I now seemed to be protecting because I thought it was special.

I asked her what she thought about the raised formations on it that, to me, looked like the Kachina and Warrior Man rock formations.

With a twinkle in her eye, she said, "If you turn it upside down, it looks like the state of Florida!" She added with a chuckle, "And here's a man who looks like he's praying."

But she wasn't teasing me, as she explained, "The rocks all around this area seem to be in *layers*. All of them. So, if they look like they are revealing something to you in their layers, that makes total sense. Something is resonating with you."

She continued, "The red rock is fascinating and rather fragile too."

Robert shapes the rocks into hearts, and that's not an easy thing to do, I started to realize. The red rock usually wants to fall apart. He must bake it, or something, some process to get it to form the heart shape and then keep its shape.

"If you see him again, you should ask him how he makes all those hearts he gives out as gifts every day. It must take him a long time."

And then she said with a smile, "So what are you going to do now, missy? You have quite a mystery on your hands. This is a discovery, and I'd love to see you keep researching it."

I told her I had no idea. I guess I could call science departments at local colleges and look for someone who might have knowledge about this. I had gone to my niece's college orientation last month, and I heard our tour guide mention that one of the professors in their science department was studying string theory. This rang a bell with me—I have always pictured the planet as a giant ball of twine—but I'm also certain that I have no idea what scientific string theory is all about.

Darlynn agreed this might be a good approach. We discussed our connections to all humans and the importance of relating to one another in a kind way. Whatever energy we put out into the world is likely what will be returned to us. In other words, what goes around comes around.

Suzan and I treasured our time with Darlynn that afternoon. We left feeling peaceful and hopeful for the future, whatever that may entail.

As she waved us goodbye, Darlynn said to me, "I hope you will decide to pursue the orbs and the rocks. I think it's pretty fascinating. I'd like to see you do something with that, but it's up to you, of course. Whether or not you want to put yourself out there, that's totally your decision. I'm always here to help if you need anything; just call me."

I was very thankful, but at that point, I had *no* idea what I would do with the orb photo. I had *no* idea if I was even interested in pursuing an acceptable explanation for the bubble on my photo.

I had to think of my family. When you decide to put yourself *out there*…to share your personal story and your information, you have to think about how it will affect everyone in your life. And it does. My daughter was in middle school at the time, my niece was in high school, and we were living in a very tight-knit community. I had to give this some considerable thought before I would decide to be referred to as the Orb Lady or the Rock Woman. (Both were labels I would earn in the years to come.)

On the positive side, you may think that only *you* are responsible for your success, but there's always someone you can thank, a teacher, a parent, or a mentor, who has given you the guidance and encouragement that you needed along the way.

Success by yourself is almost impossible; you *have* to have good people around you. Not everyone will support you and your goals and your dreams. So, you'll have to sense when you feel that connection with someone who wants the best for you. And be discerning about who you spend your time with. I feel fortunate to have the most amazing string of people in this story. Each person has unknowingly guided me to the next, significant *connection* (the next person) who would ultimately make this a story worth telling.

7

THE HEART-SHAPED ORB AT LAKE CYPRESS SPRINGS

An orb in motion!

I could barely believe it. I'd seen an orb moving.

Through some casual internet searching, I'd happened upon a video of an orb, *moving*. I contacted the person who'd posted the video, Craig, and he sent me the link to another spectacular video, and I say spectacular because his doing this meant a lot to me. I felt validated in some way, like I wasn't the only person seeing circles of light on photographs.

He wished me good luck on my exploration and told me that he was not a scientist but that he was a Christian, and based on what he had seen and video-taped, his opinion was that the orbs are something that move with intention and purpose and by their own energy.

He also suggested I check out a book entitled *The New Frontier*, by Cedar Rivers, and it was a copy of that book that arrived one morning in June 2015 when my husband and I were flying back home to Texas from visiting friends on the East Coast. That was great timing! I opened the box, put the book in my carry-on bag, and left quickly for the airport.

It was a beautiful, clear morning to fly, and to read—no turbulence. The book had a beautiful cover with green grass and trees, some blue water, and white images—circles of light! *Wow!* I said to myself, *That's it! These are the orbs that I'm seeing and photographing!* I was loving it.

Maybe this book contained exactly what I had been searching for! Maybe I would find the answers to my questions in this book, and I could rest easy knowing that other people have seen and photographed orbs, just like me, and they are perfectly fine, simple people, just like me.

I could feel that I was following the steps to discovery. One person would tell me to look at a certain website, and then the person I found there would tell me to check out a book that would lead to the next step, and so on. I loved and appreciated all of the connections swirling around me, holding me with others.

The author began by talking about the baby boomer generation, of which I am a part, by being born in 1963. In fact, the author and I were born the same year in the same month, just on opposite sides of the world. She wrote about the times of our lives, the here and now of humanity, and how we are in the midst of transforming.

OK, I thought, *I don't know anything about this.* I wasn't particularly drawn into the subject of multiple realms of existence or the ascension, which I had never heard of.

Cedar Rivers's extraordinary photographs of nature spirits—including gnomes, elves, tree spirits, and fairies—prove beyond doubt, Rivers wrote, that they are real.

Whaaaaaat? Oh my, I think I might be a little crazy; this is just a little too much for me to grasp.

I thought I was searching for a simple energy of some kind. I wasn't thinking about fairies who would be unveiling the mysteries of the multiple realms of existence! Yikes. What had I gotten myself into this time?

But as I turned the pages of her book, my skimming picked up speed, not because I was eager to be through the book but because I was hungry for more.

I couldn't believe my eyes! The author had included pages of her photographs: pictures of long streams of light, which she called *shafts*, and so many round orbs, pure-white circles of light, and colorful shapes of all sizes.

I glanced over at my husband with shock, and he was looking at his phone or computer with his headphones on. I struggled to get his attention across the center aisle, so I tossed a crumpled piece of paper into his lap. Once we made eye contact, I passed him the book and motioned to the pages he should look at.

I said, "This author has almost every single shape that I've photographed. I can't believe it—this is incredible. This is the validation that I've been searching for."

I couldn't get on board with all of the dreamy, angel-fairy things that she was talking about. I understand that she was describing her experience, and I respect that, but I also thought, *I'm not gettin' on that train!*

But there was no denying that our pictures were strikingly similar in every way, so I decided to read her story carefully, with the goal to gain some perspective about the orbs.

One of the author's suggestions about photographing orbs was to *talk to them*. I couldn't imagine that. That seemed like a completely strange suggestion to me.

But I did understand some of the suggestions, like making use of the camera's flash and going out to take pictures at significant times like sunrise and sunset, when the colors of the sky are typically more dramatic. From what I've seen, orb phenomena can appear on photographs at any time of the day or night, inside or outside, and with or without the camera's or cell phone's flash. But there are still times and ways that will help you be more likely to catch sight of an orb and get a picture or video clip of it.

She also mentioned tree spirits, numerology, synchronicity, and the ascension, which I know nothing about. But I do share the author's love of nature.

I was intrigued by this book, so I made it my goal to take some of her suggestions, put them into action, and see if I got any results.

Still, I was plagued by self-doubt and worry. It was as though the more I thought about these orbs, even the more outside confirmation I got, the more I fretted. Thoughts would enter my mind late at night when I was trying to fall asleep.

What if I wake up tomorrow, and for whatever reason, all my pictures are blank? What if I've lost my digital cards; they are empty or erased; there's no proof that I've ever photographed orbs? What if I never photograph another orb again?

I don't have to do this. I don't have to do anything. I don't have to tell anyone about the orbs. I'll just give up. Yes, that's what I'll do! I have the right to do that, and it's perfectly acceptable. I don't have to put myself out there and risk being referred to as the Orb Lady!

For as many people who have agreed there is magic in what I'm seeing, there are the same number who think I'm seeing something where there is really nothing. What I've learned about people by showing them pictures and having conversations about all of this is that, in general, people are either open to seeing new and different things or they are not.

For example, in 2007, I took several photos when it snowed the evening of December 24 in Texas. Yes, it was Christmas Eve, so anything can happen—but we rarely see snow in Texas in December. I was pretty amazed at the photos I took of our family standing at the front door with the snowfall, not just because of the snow but because of the fascinating colored circles of light all around them.

My daughter had synchro team practice at the ice rink, so I loaded the pictures on to my iPad so I could show them to my "mom friends" and get their opinion.

This was early in my adventure with the orbs, and it was my first encounter with resistance. We were all sitting at a round table, and I told the ladies that I had something interesting on my pictures. I asked them to tell me what they thought.

They said things like, "That's crazy," and, "Wow, I've never seen anything like this. What do you think it is?" Which was encouraging; actually, all but one was supportive. And then one friend said, "You need to send your camera back to the manufacturer because something's wrong with it. It's defective."

And then another lady said, "My pictures look like that."

Interesting. I thought that might be wonderful because I could have an answer! If her pictures looked exactly like mine, then mystery solved! I wouldn't have to wonder anymore, because I wasn't seeing anything novel or extraordinary.

And then she said, "Yes, when we go to Colorado during the winter to ski, that's what snow looks like on my pictures."

Hmmm. Not exactly the response I was hoping for, but maybe she was misinterpreting what she saw. I said, "Oh, that's great. Well, can you bring your pictures to the rink so that I can see them? Honestly, I'm really trying to figure this out."

She never brought her photos to the rink. I'm guessing what she meant by "my pictures look like that" was that I was being silly, and I didn't really have anything out of the ordinary. Also that I was reading too much into the photos. That the circles were nothing more than simple reflections or dust on the camera's lens. "My pictures look like that" was ultimately a putdown. It was the first of many putdowns that I would encounter on this journey.

I have since realized then that a large percentage of my viewing audience might always refuse to recognize something that I feel is truly fascinating. The orbs might always be dust, pollen, water, or reflections to some people, no matter how they appear on a photograph. The real, physical evidence of pictures will never change some people's minds. So, this adventure with orbs is also teaching me about people. The way people think, the way that they process what they see in this world.

People seem to pick and choose data that supports the opinions that they already have. As with our political process, typically, each voter is supposed to choose a side. But when you're on a side, I think you lose the openness to consider.

Think about the difference in this example.

Someone might say, "I can't vote for this person because they're not on my side." In fact, that's something we commonly say!

But one time my cousin Patricia asked me, "Well, could you at least *consider* voting for this person?"

And I really thought about it. The way she phrased her question made me sincerely think about who I would vote for.

Politics is an entirely different can of worms from orbs, but that example helps me explain the reactions I receive from others. Some things that happen in this world unite us, and other things divide us.

It was a challenge at first when I shared some of the photos on social media. Many people think that orbs are mysterious and interesting and not a bad thing. It's great to have that support. But there are some very hateful people who write terrible things, and they get the chain of ridicule started, and others want to laugh and join in. They have the freedom to have their thoughts, and I definitely have the freedom to avoid people who are only looking for an argument or a debate. We can agree to disagree.

Orbs on photos can be very subtle, which is why many people haven't noticed them. Sometimes one orb appears, and sometimes there are multiple orbs on a single photo. Sometimes an orb is perfectly circular with bright, white light in the middle, glowing warm colors on one side and perfectly balanced cool colors on the other side. Sometimes the orbs take on a different shape, as I've seen with heart shapes and what I call blobs.

A good example would be the photo I took of a dog that always ran around loose at the lake, and he would sit on our deck. His name was Bordeaux, and he was a very sweet dog. I don't know how I got close enough to see his tag, I didn't pet him, but he would come around every day when we would visit the lake. We were outside on the deck, and I took a picture of him with a large, glowing mass of light over his head.

I also know I can believe what I know to be true: that what I see, and photograph, are real. The images on my photos were not fabricated or created in an app, not in any way. I realize that many people would tell me that all the images on my pictures are, in their opinion, really *nothing*.

Nothing meaning they are dust, snow, reflections, headlights, rain or any kind of condensation, or bugs. But I don't have to believe them, and that is the key.

Today, as I am writing this, it is the birthday of my dear sister, Sue. I will miss her laughter for as long as I live here without her. She was a light in this world. I just had a notification that a favorite quote of hers posted, so I looked at it. This quote, by Dr. Wayne Dyer, arrived perfectly timed with her birthday and perfectly timed with my writing at this exact moment.

It goes like this:

The ultimate ignorance is the rejection of something you know nothing about yet refuse to investigate.

So, as you can tell, I had a lot of conflicting thoughts and feelings and fears and certainty swirling around my mind. I had to give this some serious thought. Incidentally, I have since learned from publishers at Hay House that Dr. Wayne Dyer was a big believer of orbs on photographs. He even requested that if anyone captured an orb with him in a photo when he was speaking at a conference, they please send him the photo. I was so happy to hear that because, as many people have, I've read his books and watched him speak on public television throughout the years.

I think of his peaceful spirit and how we are on God's time, and we have to trust that. Our existence here is beautiful, and precious, and fragile. It took me ten years of dating after college to find the man that I wanted to spend my life with (and, believe me, that felt like a lifetime when I was in my twenties); it took me just the right amount of time to believe in the orbs and to believe in myself regarding the orbs.

One word: *trust*. Be patient and trust that our lives play out exactly the way they should, whatever that may be.

Well, when I was stuck in that quandary a few years ago, what better place to ponder all of that than at the lake! My family and I began packing for an extended weekend camping and fishing with friends at our vacation home on Lake Cypress Springs, one hundred miles from home. After searching for a few years at different lakes around the metroplex, we found a cute little green house on a cove in the country.

When you live in a city and you love nature, the way I do, there are so many wonderful things about spending a weekend in the country, including all the wildlife we see (and try not to surprise!), like deer and foxes. We spend a lot more time cooking together there too, and we log a lot less screen time! Every now and then, one of the kids' friends or our cousins will look for a better Wi-Fi connection in the area, but after a few hours, their attention is usually diverted away from their cell phones.

Today's drive was beautiful. It was July, but it had rained for a few days, so it was still pretty cool, meaning that we hadn't hit triple digits for the summer.

The excitement usually builds when we exit the highway at mile marker 146, sometimes stopping at the Dairy Queen (OK, always stopping at the Dairy Queen), and then we drive the twists and turns of the country roads that take us to Wilcox, and we are home, at the lake!

So many times, we've arrived to find a family of deer or a family of foxes in our front yard. It's also fascinating how some animals can dig a hole in the ground and make a nice den for themselves, either underneath the earth or underneath our deck. I've seen rabbit holes in our backyard. I once pulled back a flap of green grass and found a litter of baby bunnies! It was crazy.

They were hidden but also right there underneath the grass.

I always have that feeling of excitement just to get there and open up the house. Our home away from home! The house sits on an acre lot where our dogs love to run. Everything looked so green. During the summer, the grass grows very quickly, and you almost need to mow it more than once a week. Thankfully, our mower, Nash, had recently taken care of the yard, so everything looked perfect.

We unpacked the cars, everyone got comfortable in their rooms and put their swimsuits on, and my daughter, Sarah, and her friend, Kenzie, headed to the dock with their beach bags. Sarah and Kenzie are on a synchronized figure skating team together called the Texas All Stars. When we had the team visit for a weekend, the girls were all awake and on the boat dock at sunrise because they all meet at the ice rink to skate at 6:00 a.m. five days a week.

I'll also never forget the first morning I woke up to the rumble of a high-powered motor. At the crack of dawn. *What in the world?* I thought. Was it an earthquake? A helicopter or airplane? What on earth was creating this earth-shattering sound?

It was then we discovered that apparently ten feet from the corner of our boat dock resided one of the best-known, and most popular, crappie holes on the lake! If you fish for crappie, I guess that's a really big deal. The fishing boats wait in line for a spot at this incredible fishing spot. That has been another learning experience for me.

I've learned an appreciation for fishing and the nuances of the sport as I understand that some types of fish, the crappie included, are temperamental, meaning that they require of fishers a fair amount of knowledge and experience to produce a successful catch. I've grown to respect the art of fishing.

We have a townhome in the city, so we do many things in the country that we don't normally do at home. Like wash the windows, go fishing, mop the floors, jump on the trampoline, go fishing, chop firewood, and did I say, go fishing?

Back to this particular weekend at the lake. Mike was power-washing the boat dock, and I was picking up pinecones and branches in the yard. The girls were cleaning the dust off the furniture, setting up their hammocks, and blowing leaves off the deck and driveway when Mike's phone rang. It was Nash.

"Hey, I needed to give you a call because I know that you are arriving today," he said. "I had a little emergency, and I'm so sorry that I couldn't get my yards mowed this week."

Mike didn't understand. He said, "Nash, the yard looks great. I'm so sorry to hear that something's wrong, though. Are you OK?"

Nash explained he'd cut his hand and needed stitches but was fine.

Mike of course didn't bother to ask why our grass looked like it had been recently mowed.

He just said, "No worries. The grass looks fine. We can see you in a couple of weeks." Mike told him to take care, but wasn't sure if he should mention the fact that our lawn had been mysteriously mowed, and by whom?

As we were picking up some tree branches in the backyard, I noticed that our new next-door neighbor, Linda, had family in town too, though I hadn't yet met them. She had purchased the property from the previous owner's family when he passed away. I didn't pay much attention to her construction, but I do remember seeing a pile of trash on the driveway. All of the items that had to be cleared out to build a new interior, a new home for Linda. It was sobering to see Phil's personal items, like books, dishes, and coffee mugs, in a pile of trash waiting to be hauled away. It made me sad, but it also made me feel some perspective. You really can't take anything with you when you leave this world. That's just reality. Everything that we can see will go away someday.

Later in the afternoon, Mike told me that he'd been talking with Tim and learned Tim had mowed our yard. Tim, it turned out, was Linda's son-in-law.

"Wow, that's nice." I said. "I mean, who just mows someone else's yard for them? And it's not exactly a small yard."

Most people wouldn't do that for a neighbor they'd never met before. I was so moved by his gesture that I searched around for something I could offer him and his family, but I really didn't have anything nice to give them.

I searched through my duffel bag. I had various types of

batteries, digital cards, and camera equipment. Nope, nothing. The only item in my bag that had any value or personal significance to me was the heart-shaped rock that Robert had given to me in the canyon on my fiftieth birthday.

I picked it up and held it with both of my hands. It was rough, but that's what was great about it. The rock had a slight heaviness to it, but the shape of the heart was so cool. I was thinking that this might be the one thing, the one unique item that would be perfect for Tim. I felt a little strange about this, and could I really part with something so special?

I thought, *Oh my gosh, he's going to think I'm such a weirdo.* I pondered the risk. I considered that he took a risk by mowing our lawn, unsolicited—what if we hadn't wanted it mowed?—and he hadn't even met us yet.

And this rock had been given to me in a surprise moment, so now it could be the perfect way to continue the kindness and pass it on. I sat and prayed, and I waited for an answer… and the answer was *Absolutely! Pass the gift of the rock to the next person because he has earned it with his random act of kindness.* I'm a person who's much more likely to pass something to the next person rather than hang on to everything.

My friends and I have always done that with books and movies. When I loan them out, instead of asking for it to be returned, I tell the person, "I don't need it back; just pass it to the next person."

Yes, I decided the rock was the perfect gift to offer. Well, almost. I found a file and some scrubbing pads, and I smoothed the edges and filed down some of the rough spots. I guess I wanted to put my own touch on it.

I looked out the window and saw people sitting on Linda's dock. I had a hand-written thank-you note and the heart-shaped rock, so I walked next door, down their driveway, and through their yard to where they were sitting.

As I approached, I said, "Hello, Linda! I'm looking for the person who may have mowed our yard next door. Do you know anything about that?"

One of the men sitting there answered, "That's me. I hope you don't mind. I was just bored and thought it might be nice if you were coming out anytime soon to have your yard looking nice when you got here."

I told him that I thought that was incredibly nice of him and that we really appreciated what he did. I told him that we could pay him for the mow. He said, "No, no way." He didn't want that.

I said, "Well, I wanted to give you something." I held out the rock. "A man gave it to me while I was in Arizona, and I thought it was so nice of him, so I wanted to pass it along to you, to show our appreciation for what you did."

Tim was curious as he looked at the rock in his hands. I was a little nervous waiting to see what his reaction would be.

He said, "A heart? Wow. That's cool. Well, thank you. Let me introduce you to my wife, Jill." Jill was sitting in a rocking chair farther up the dock, closer to the water's edge. The sun was just starting to set, and it looked like we would see some dramatic colors reflecting off the water tonight.

As we walked up the dock, Tim continued, "Jill was just

released from the Baylor Heart Hospital, so we brought her out here to recover. She just had heart surgery."

I said, "Oh my gosh, wow. How's she doing?"

Tim said, "Her procedure went well. She seems to be doing great, but she has to take it easy for a while."

Tim and I were both a little surprised by the connection of the heart. I said hello to Jill, and she told me about the valve replacement she had at the hospital.

It was endoscopic surgery, not open-heart, so the doctors had high expectations for her recovery. I was amazed and surprised by the day, and I thought about how moved I was by this random act of kindness.

These days, in our society, it can be rare to enjoy a day when a good Samaritan takes it upon themselves to do something nice for a friend or for a stranger.

The reality is there are so many good people in the world who would jump at the chance to help someone in need, whether it was a friend or a stranger. We just don't see as many of those stories covered in the media.

The evening was approaching, and the girls were cooking dinner sides and dessert in the kitchen. Mike and I were grilling outside, and I suddenly remembered that, just for fun, I was going to take pictures the way that the author of *The New Frontier*, Cedar Rivers, recommended.

I went inside and got my camera. It was almost dusk, and I was standing still outside, looking at the water and appreciating the day and the beautiful evening that was unfolding. I took pictures facing the boat dock, and I saw large white specks in a line on several of the pictures. It looked as though the white circles were following each other. They were swirling around sort of in a pattern. I thought, *Bugs.*

I turned toward the back of our house—everyone was inside by now—and I took a series of photos.

One picture, and then another of our garden and trampoline in the backyard. At this point, I could hear the advice from Rivers's book in my head: *Talk to them.*

"Talk to who?" I said to myself. "This is silly. Sandy, you've really lost your marbles this time."

I paused.

Reluctantly, I murmured under my breath, "OK, look. I don't know what this is, but if you're out there, by any chance, I just want to say thank you. That's all I'm thinking. I'm just thankful if you're around, if you're watching us. I don't know."

All the time I was speaking, I was thinking this might be ridiculous, but I was trying it anyway.

I raised the camera to my face, but instead of looking through the viewfinder, I chose to watch over the garden instead.

As I pressed the shutter-release button, I extended my arm out in front of me. I wanted to see if I could actually see any orbs, if they were to appear. There was a huge flash of white light. My eyes were wide open, and I couldn't believe what I saw. In fact, I thought, there was no way that I had just seen what flashed on my camera. I stood there for a moment in the dark, looking around to see if anyone was outside watching me.

I didn't see anyone. The sun had just set, and I could hear

the sound of a light breeze blowing through the trees. I could see Mike, Sarah, Kenzie, and our dogs in the kitchen inside the house.

I quickly turned the camera to review mode, and I looked at the photos I had just taken. There were orbs, many of them all-white, swirling together in a line.

And then there was what looked like a giant, white heart shape floating over the trampoline.

I couldn't believe it. I was in shock. I stopped taking photos and ran inside to show everyone. They were all busy, and they didn't really care what I was doing. *Yeah, that's Mom, taking her silly pictures.*

I was so excited I didn't know what it meant, but I thought if the light looked like a heart, it must mean something. What in the world were these mysterious orbs? What was this phenomenon? Who was this? I had so many questions and no answers.

I said, "You guys, look, look at this!" I showed them the review screen on my camera, and Kenzie said, "It's a heart!" Mike and Sarah said, "Oh yeah, that's nice."

As long as I live, I will always be thankful to Kenzie, who was willing to play along and entertain this historic moment with me. She has a special place in my heart.

What do you do when you see something that's out of the ordinary? Something you think might be profoundly significant? The younger generation would immediately say, "Instagram it!" I didn't, because I wasn't on Instagram or any social media at that time.

I continued to take photos of the little green house with orbs floating around it.

In one, Mike is sitting in the backyard with a huge orb floating over the campfire. I have photographed an orb that looks exactly like this one in different locations, so I'm beginning to wonder if it's the same orb. I may never know.

I wasn't sure what I'd witnessed with the appearance of the heart-shaped orb, but I felt as if I'd seen a miracle. The picture has other circles of hot-white light around it, but the one large image of the heart is spectacular. Why the shape of the heart? Why wasn't it shaped like a cross or a star or a moon?

The heart is one thing that every human being has in common. I guess you could say that about any organ in the body, but the white light didn't appear in the shape of a liver, kidney, lung, or brain. I realized that the heart is the universally accepted symbol of love.

When we returned home, I started my search for information about orbs and heart-shaped orbs. I called the science departments at local colleges and universities. Basically, what I was told was that they didn't have classes for the study of orbs or strange phenomena on photographs because there weren't any jobs in that field.

So much for my new, fascinating hobby. It seems to be that there's a small percentage of people who are actually familiar with the word *orbs*, and it's my opinion that no one truly knows what orbs are, so the topic is a bit of a dead end as far as research goes.

I sat on our back porch and emailed the heart-shaped orb photo to Darlynn in Sedona. She was my sounding board, and I needed her advice.

Her response was "This is extraordinary. Sandy, this is a real game-changer."

Great, I thought, *What does that mean?*

Darlynn explained, "It means that this is different. Many of us have been seeing orbs for years, but when you have a photograph such as this, with its significant shape, and 'the story behind it' looks like the universe is responding to you, or to something in the environment, and that's truly exciting! You have to do something with this, whether it's a blog or an article, or maybe a book. I think you should share this story. Also, make sure you search through your family photos; you might find more orbs on your photos that you've never realized existed."

I had to be honest with her, I wasn't sure how or why I would tell this story. There's usually a reason why we do the things we do. Whenever I produced a video at work, I would begin with the question "Why do we need this video?"

To define our purpose, our goal, we must answer questions:

Who is our audience, and what do we want them to learn after watching this? Is it for educational purposes or to simply communicate a message?

What was my purpose with this?

8

September in Newtown, Connecticut, and October in Oconee, Georgia

> "What is the secret of your life?" asked Mrs. Browning of Charles Kingsley; "Tell me, that I may make mine beautiful too?" He replied, "I had a friend."
>
> William C. Gannet

This chapter is about the rare and special people we are lucky enough to call friends. In my case, I'm particularly lucky I know people who will walk alongside me on this journey. These are the people in my life who, when life pulls us in so many directions, instinctively say, "I'll go with you." I have several friends who immediately connected with my story and were not only supportive of my efforts but also encouraging all along the way. Three of them asked me to speak at their book club meetings, which was so generous of them and provided a unique opportunity for me to connect with people and experience the spontaneous conversations that arise in a live setting.

When you attempt to write a true story, there are several factors to consider. Writing takes time away from your family, time that you will never get back. You have to confront your fears and self-doubt almost daily, and it takes a lot of perseverance. Maybe writing is easy for some people, but it's not easy for me. My friends' support has been integral to this journey happening and to me then recounting it.

Take, for example, my friend Lisa. The Sunday we returned home from our incredible weekend at Lake Cypress Springs, we found my friend Lisa in the midst of making us a gift—she was crafting us a fall wreath for our front door! But soon she'd be giving me much more, help finding orbs in old photographs.

I thought of an old wreath we had stored in the attic that she could use to build our new wreath from, so we both climbed up the ladder to look for it. It wasn't a surprise that we had stacks of boxes marked "old photos."

I couldn't wait to start looking for orbs on our photos, so we hauled the boxes downstairs and set them in a row. We looked inside a few of the boxes, and they were full of hundreds of photos from decades ago.

After Lisa and I gathered all of the materials for the wreath, it was getting too late to start the search, so I set a date for Friday night, and I invited four more friends to join us and look through photos. Why would they do this, you might ask? Because I offered a wine-tasting and charcuterie to go with it, of course!

We sat at a large, round table and each had our wine, snacks, and a box of photos. Donna had a box marked, "Samantha," which had photos I had taken of my niece starting in 1995.

Kris had an older box, which had photos dating back to when I was in high school in 1980. I also had Margie, Kelly, Lori, Kris, and Brandy searching through so many piles of photos that we ended up sitting all over the floor.

We had to keep boxes marked that were already searched so we didn't repeat the process again. We only separated specific photos that had anything out of the ordinary pictured on the photo. The search party was fun, and our efforts produced a pile of fifty or sixty photos that sparked our curiosity.

We separated the "here's something that looks strange" pile into seven more piles, each with similar looking phenomena on them. One pile was "snow"; another was "orange streaks"; and another was "photos with orange circles that have a cross in the middle."

It felt like we were putting the pieces of a puzzle together, but we had no box lid to consult. We had no grand map or instructions to explain the meaning of the mystery. The pictures that sparked the most debate were the photos of Samantha, Sarah, and their cousins with large circles of white light all around them, and there appeared to be snow on the ground.

The orbs were spectacular, in different colors and mostly round shapes, in addition to the white circles of light.

Some say that this is definitely a reflection off the snow, but I also have photos that I've taken when it *was* snowing, and all you see are *flakes*, not round balls of light. So, my question is, "Can snowflakes form the shape of a big, round ball?"

So many opinions on this and so much debate.

The orange streams of light that occur on several photos are curious. We found six photos from different years, different places, and even different cameras. Every photo has an orange stream on it in the exact same location. Four of the six photos show the orange stream in the upper-right-hand corner of the photo. There is one with Samantha, another with a picture of me with my sister, Sue. Another with an orange ray of light over Samantha as a baby, while her parents are holding her. Yet another with Samantha as a toddler when she is visiting us at our home in Texas. The curious stream of orange light is also next to her as a child, and there's a newspaper that's on the dresser behind her. The similarity in the orange stream photos is uncanny.

*

Another friend I think of fondly is Karen. I remember the first time I met Karen, at my sister's home. Sue was having a neighborhood gathering, and I answered her front door for her. There stood the woman I'd soon know as my friend Karen. There aren't many people for whom I can recall the details of our first meeting, but Karen is one such person.

As this stranger stood before me at my sister's door, she was strikingly familiar—the person you just can't figure out where you've seen them before, yet you know you have. Suddenly, I knew. Karen looks exactly like Julia Roberts. Of course! How lucky for her! Does she get mistaken for the famous actor? Yes, sometimes, but there is only one Karen, just like each individual is unique on this earth. Research proves that no two of us are alike, not even identical twins, according to new genetic research.

In 2016, years after we met, I would visit Karen and her family in Connecticut for the weekend. She and her son, Alex, were so kind to pick me up at LaGuardia, and then it was a beautiful evening to drive from New York City to Connecticut.

At a lull in what had been our nonstop catching up, Karen said, "Hey, do you want to see the new Sandy Hook Elementary School? Did you bring your camera?"

Karen had appreciated the orb photos I had shared with her, so she already had that on her radar, and in this case, she was one step ahead of me. I hadn't even thought about how close I'd be to this emotional site. And of course I had my 35mm camera with me. It was the one I typically used to take pictures while on vacation. It was also the camera that had captured some of the orb photos so far.

The streets in Connecticut are so beautiful in September, the way they twist and turn underneath the trees. As I prepared myself for what I was about to see, I appreciated the beauty of the widely spaced houses with big yards and lots of green space and the refreshing feel of the cool air.

It was almost sunset when Karen, Alex, and I arrived at the new school. As we stepped out of the car, I noticed teenagers playing on a nearby baseball field. Otherwise, the space was quiet that Friday evening.

The new building has a lot of wood in its design; it's very beautiful, and it looks somewhat like a church cathedral with its windows and a weathervane on the roof. I noticed the pretty yellow flowers dotting the property, and I thought about all the teachers and the children on that fateful Friday of December 14, 2012.

Over fifteen hundred miles from Newtown, Connecticut, my mom was the substitute nurse that day at my daughter Sarah's elementary school in McKinney, Texas. I was a volunteer assistant for the day. Windows along a short hallway gave us a clear view from the nurse's office to the main office, so we could see staff members running back and forth to answer the phones. And the phones were ringing! Our office staff members seemed to be scrambling, and then it seemed like we suddenly had a lot of students being signed out for the day.

I popped my head out into the hallway to ask one of the secretaries rushing by, "Hey, what's going on?"

She answered, "There's been a mass shooting at an elementary school in Connecticut, and it's not good."

No, it was horrific, and the events that day, two weeks before Christmas, would turn out to be the worst mass shooting at an elementary school in US history.

Now, almost four years later, the three of us were standing in the parking lot of this place newly reclaimed by its community. I lifted my camera to my face. When I am looking for orbs, I start by taking a series of photos to capture the landscape, in this case, the front of the school. Taking pictures of this building probably wouldn't raise the suspicions of any passerby. To them, I'd look to be just taking in the new design.

We walked to the front door and peeked inside. There is a

large, beautiful, green mosaic piece on the wall that reads: "Be Kind." We then walked to our left on the walkway that goes around the school.

I focused my camera on the back corner of the school and pressed the shutter-release button. I took a photo pointed toward the sky, and the flash went off. The picture is fairly dark, but there is a curious circle of light in the upper-right-hand corner of the photo. I didn't see anything in the sky at the time I took the photo.

Sunset was almost over. The next photo lights up the foreground, which shows two gray posts, the water hose, and the sprinkler running at the bottom of the photo. There are tiny balls of light in the distance. On the next photo, there are three circles of light that are visible, still in the upper-right-hand corner of the photo.

Still, I didn't see anything in the moment with my naked eye. Karen and Alex were behind me about thirty feet. I said to Karen, "I don't think I'm getting anything. I don't see much." She nodded and followed Alex back toward the front of the school. I decided to hang back for just a moment and repeat what I did at the lake, which seemed to result in the photo of the heart-shaped orb.

I spoke to the orbs.

It felt very awkward, the same as it did the first time I spoke to them, but I was thinking of all those precious, innocent children who left their bodies right there on the ground where I was standing.

I whispered, "Hello, dear ones." I waited a moment and then pressed the shutter-release button on my camera.

The flash went off, and the sky lit up with circles of white light in various shapes and sizes! The sky suddenly changed and was now covered with orbs.

The top of the water droplets from the sprinkler on the ground are visible at the bottom of the picture.

Naysayers will always say that these are reflections of water, dust, anything you can imagine in the atmosphere. But if you take a closer look at any of the orbs in the photo, you will see a ring of glowing light around each; one half is cool colors, and the other half is warm colors like orange and yellow. Also, there is a distinctive "spot" inside each orb.

I took three more photos at the corner of the school that night, and they all show multiple orbs spread across the sky.

What a great idea Karen had to visit the school and appreciate its new design and remember the innocent victims of the Sandy Hook shooting.

After we left the school, we stopped at an Italian restaurant and picked up dinner to take back to Karen's home. While Karen was talking to the servers about our order, I had a moment to talk with the host. I told her that we went to see the new school, and she told me it was somewhat of a tourist attraction. Many people wanted to see what the new design would look like. Some residents weren't completely sure that the city should have built on the original footprint of the school, but nevertheless, there was a beautiful building there now.

I asked her, "What was it like that day?"

"What was it like that day?" she asked softly, clearly thinking back for a long moment. Then she said, "You know, I think the school was just swarmed with angels. So many angels. The streets were lined with TV trucks and satellite dishes. Reporters were everywhere, interviewing anyone who would talk to them. It wasn't a day that this city has ever seen, I'll tell you that." I told her I couldn't even begin to imagine.

It's staggering to think of the ripple effect that we experienced that day. Parents across the country wanted to immediately pick up their kids from school. They just wanted to hug them and take them safely home.

How powerful are the actions of one person who picks up a gun? Their actions are felt all across the country, even the world. That is collective suffering.

We are all tiny little pieces in this mosaic existence. Whether we like it or not, we have to deal with each other.

I enjoyed dinner with Karen and her family, and then she asked if I'd like to use her computer to look at my pictures. It took some effort, with different computers and a different camera to upload from, but we finally got the photos transferred, and we were able to view them on a bigger screen. Her husband, also named Mike, looked at the pictures of the orbs all over the sky and said, "See, that's water." He meant they weren't anything out of the ordinary, just droplets of water from the sprinkler. I understood where he was coming from, but based on what I had seen, I knew that the circles in the sky were something special.

I answered, "I get that, but I know what I saw. I know that there wasn't anything on the first frame and then what appeared on the next three or four frames. I think this is actually a great representation of orbs in the sky with water at the bottom of the picture. The water sprinkler is actually perfect for the picture; it offers a nice comparison."

Mike nodded and then shook his head.

Karen and I winked at each other, knowing that everybody has the right to believe what they want. Every person has the right to their opinion.

*

One fall, my friend Amy, who is a singer-songwriter based in rural Tennessee, decided to host a "creative conference" in her home state of Georgia. I love the fall season anywhere in the US. Temperatures are mild, the trees are changing colors, some states more colorful than others, and it's a very exciting time leading up to some of the traditional holidays and family gatherings.

So, it felt like exactly the right time to do some creating under Amy's wise guidance. While packing for this long weekend, I spied my second heart-shaped rock, given to me by Robert when I had traveled to Sedona months earlier with Suzan. I accepted his gift because I had already regifted the first one he gave me, to my neighbor at the lake.

Well, seeing that rock, I wondered, *Should I take this with me?* Of course the answer was yes! There were several of us joining Amy at Oconee Lake, and if I felt that I needed to give this rock to someone this weekend, it might be interesting to see if the giving might produce another interesting photo.

The first night of the conference was very social, everyone mixing and mingling with cocktails and street tacos. I took some photos and captured an orb floating over another photographer's head.

We watched an artist named Jimmy paint a beautiful landscape of Amy's barn back in Tennessee, and we also watched a video about him. It was impressive and emotional because Jimmy is legally blind.

It was a humbling experience to watch him paint and an enjoyable evening of music and camaraderie. The attendees were people who wanted to learn about the creative process—many of us are in jobs that don't call for us to tell stories, paint pictures, or perform music. We were also all carrying challenges, like loss of friends and family or personal chronic illness.

We realized this clearly during the second session of the first day, The Tree of Me. We gathered in a room with ten round tables, but when it was time to get to work, most of us found a place to sit on the floor.

Instructor Cindy Hudson guided each of us through drawing a tree on a large piece of paper. This exercise provided a time for introspection and was designed to give answers to basic questions about each of us from the most important source, which is us. Topics ranged from the physical, emotional, and spiritual to time and money and relationships.

This class would cover a lot of ground for each person!

As I drew my tree, I gave sincere thought to so many facets of my life. The class was giving me a positive perspective on all the life experiences I've had in this world. I learned that being available to my own wisdom and what works for me gives me the ability to set strong boundaries around toxic situations, navigate vulnerability, and choose what is best for me.

I had never met Cindy before this conference, but after I reviewed my photos from an event at Amy's farm approximately one year earlier, I realized that Cindy was in one of the photos I had taken near the barn, and that photo shows a large orb at the top of the stairs. With the class discussion centered around living fearlessly, promoting kindness, and operating from your heart, I decided that Cindy must be the recipient of the heart-shaped rock that I was carrying in my camera bag. With encouragement from Amy, who agreed over coffee later that day that the rock would be an absolutely perfect gift for Cindy, the matter was settled.

Around fifty of us gathered the next morning on the front steps of the lakeside house to take a group photo. When I look at that photo today, I feel so much love for each and every new friend

I got to know that weekend. It's funny how kids today take an enormous number of photos with their cell phones, but are they really capturing special moments? I don't need orbs to recognize the specialness of each moment.

After our picture, I went to chat with Cindy on the back deck. I told her the story about Robert and his gifts of carefully shaped red rock that he gives to travelers in the canyon.

I said that I was certain that the heart-shaped rock was meant for her. Not surprisingly, she loved it! As we walked down to the lake for the next class, she said, "Do you have one of my cards?" I told her no. Cindy said, "Oh, you're going to love this."

I took the business card from her. It reads: "Changing the stories you tell yourself…changes *you*." And pictured in the center is a red, sedimentary, heart-shaped rock with very simple hand-drawn wings.

It is an absolutely perfect match for the rock that I offered to her.

Cindy took this message to heart, and she felt a validation that what she was doing by coaching and teaching others to live without fear was honored and appreciated. That night, she later told me, she gathered all the teachers in the lake house and told them the story of the matching hearts. Everyone got a kick out of the serendipitous encounter of the weekend.

The last event of the weekend was an outdoor breakfast with music, stories, and prayers for the future. As we all parted ways to travel home, Cindy gave me a piece of crystal that she carried close to her heart, to wish me well until we would meet again in Texas or in Tennessee.

Cindy and I work together now, even though we live 650 miles apart. Distance means nothing in our future world of living and working through the internet, FaceTime, and Zoom calls!

The most important thing I learned from Cindy was to trust. To trust in so many things: my mission in life, my message, and my talents. And, of course, to follow my heart. Though I may have already been figuring that out…

9

MOVING FORWARD

It is the middle of August, and my daughter, Sarah, is starting her freshman year at the University of Texas in Austin. Her twenty-three-year-old cousin Samantha flew in from Philadelphia to help us move Sarah into her dorm and visit friends and family all over the hill country in the process. So, within a matter of days, as we left Sarah in her Super Target–styled dorm room and took Samantha to the airport so she could fly back to Philly, I lost two young women who are very close to me. As I hugged Samantha goodbye, she and I made a pact that we would sign up for the ten-mile Rocky Run, an annual event in downtown Philadelphia. When I returned home, I promptly scheduled my travel for November and started my training with walking around the track behind Sarah's elementary school.

She and I walked to this school every day for six years, yet since we moved out of the neighborhood, I don't know anyone on this street anymore. I feel like I'm lost in time. This is a time of great change not only for our family but for the world. Change is difficult for people because our brains are wired to perform the same tasks every day, over and over again. People don't like change because we're used to our routines, which give us a sense of security. But change, in and of itself, is good. I'm a believer in change. That reminds me of my sister's favorite quote of all time, by Albert Einstein: "Insanity is doing the same thing over and over again and expecting different results."

As I walk onto the track behind the school, I'm already sweating like a super-cold glass of sweet tea in August! I'd better remember to bring a towel with me tomorrow and also something to soak up the sweat underneath my Apple watch (I sweat so much that my wrist is wet underneath my watch), as my plan is to run my laps every day until November.

I've just started to listen to the *Rocky* soundtrack through my ear buds. This is a version stored in my iTunes, but I originally bought the album when I was thirteen years old, and I still have it. I feel good. I miss my girl in Austin, and I miss my girl in Philadelphia, but all I can see from the track is that it's a beautiful day.

At the back corner of the school, next to the park, there once was a garden brimming with vegetables, herbs, and flowers. Now, I see, it's a dried-up, brown, and withered site. Wow, it's all brown and over-grown twigs and dead foliage, it looks awful. My curiosity makes me walk up to the school and ring the bell for entry.

I don't know the current office staff, so I say, "Hi, I'm Sandy Mayberry. My daughter went to school here for many years. I was just walking by and saw the gardens in the back of the school. What happened to them?"

The ladies look at each other in a very puzzled way, and one of them says, "Oh, um…I'm not sure. Here, let me check—I'll call the principal."

Over the phone she says, "Yes, I have this lady in the office, and she's asking about the gardens out back?" There is a pause and the murmur of the principal speaking to her in her ear. "She wants to know what happened to them?" I stand and watch her listen to some more undetectable chatter. "OK, I'll tell her, thanks." The secretary hangs up and says to me, "The teacher who built those gardens as a club project for the kids left years ago, and no one wants to deal with them now because they cost money to maintain, and we don't have that kind of money in the budget."

"Oh, oh my," I say. "Well, that's too bad. I mean, for everyone. They don't look good." She apparently has no response, so she gives me a very funny look, like, I have three heads!

The wheels in my head are turning as we look at each other, both of us waiting for…something. I say, "So, who would I need to talk to—I know the gardens are on school property—if I wanted to get a crew and clean them up?"

She looks at me and then says, "I guess you'd start with the principal and then maybe the school district. Here's her address; send her an email." We still look at each other. She says, "She's not here right now."

I smile inwardly at that obvious fib, but I say, "Thank you, thanks so much. I'll be in touch."

Here's the thing: when it comes to orbs, we can always see reflections or dust or malfunctions, or we can look for the clues that prove something extraordinary moves among us. Just as I could have walked on by that abandoned garden, chalking it up as a permanent eyesore, or I could do as I did: see it as a new project worth my time and care.

I choose, if their telltale signs are there, to believe that orbs exist. They have improved my life so much, most notably making me more open-minded and pointing out the myriad connections that hold us all a part of this ball of string we twirl through the universe on.

I think about the time my friend Lisa Porter and I sat down over a glass of wine to look at each other's photos. This was after she had seen one of my impressive orb photos and exclaimed that she had a very similar photograph. She showed me several pictures with her daughter and the orbs. She also had photos of mothers and grandmothers pictured with orbs, so it looked apparent that the orbs had visited several generations of her family. I was shocked at the similarity to my photos with my mother, niece, and daughter.

Lisa had a picture of her daughter Lizzie as a young girl with a vibrant, orange stream running across the photo horizontally, but the bright-orange color with a patch of yellow was also, somehow, behind her. It's an extraordinary photo.

I showed her all the photos I had found that depicted orange streams, and all of mine appeared in the picture vertically. It was amazing—we seemed to be assembling another puzzle piecing our two families together.

Lisa grew up in Ohio, and I grew up in California, Wisconsin, and Indiana, and now we both live in the same community in Texas. Just think, there could be people all over the world—there probably are people all over this planet—who have orbs on their family photos.

For every amazing photo we looked at, I had a strikingly similar photo. We were seeing a whole new puzzle emerge from our photos as we looked at each matching picture.

Lisa would show me a photo of herself from 1980 with an orb, and I could show her a similar photo of me in the same kind of wood-paneled family room, with a circular orb floating next to me.

She has several amazing photos of her niece kneeling next to her grandmother, who is seated in a wheelchair. There are circles of white light surrounding the two of them, and on one photo, it looks like there are wings behind the little girl's back.

These pictures look like a photo I have of my husband with our daughter and her cousins, and there's a circle of white light around him. I have other photos of Mike alone and with my dad, walking in the green grass, and there are circles of orange light near them. If you take a closer look, you can see the shape of a cross inside the orange circles of light.

Orbs even seem to reflect me back to me. I've noticed that the most spectacular orb photos I've taken indicated something that was going on in my life. The orbs seemed to be responding to my thoughts with colors. For example, the first Christmas after my sister's death, we also were without her husband and their daughter because he had been diagnosed with cancer and the two of them had moved back to his hometown of Philadelphia for his treatments. Needless to say, thinking about the three empty chairs at the holiday table, I was feeling a little blue. I picked up my camera and went outside to distract myself.

As though the universe knew I needed a sign of friendship, I saw two rabbits sitting together. Rabbits crack me up because they think if they sit still and act like statues, I won't see them. So, I took a few pictures of the bunnies. Then I turned and took another photo—at nothing, really, I thought. Sometimes I'll just take a picture of our street in hopes that I'll capture something interesting, so I turned to my left, and I took a picture.

I couldn't believe my eyes when I looked at the photo later. I hadn't seen anything in the sky, and yet there was a very large, beautiful blue orb in my next-door neighbor's front yard. This orb is a spectacular image, with several rings around its edges and yellow/orange warm colors on the bottom and blue/green cool colors on the top.

It has the signature "little circle" inside it, and there's also another large, transparent orb in the upper-right-hand corner of the photo. Again, I was dumbfounded by what I'd captured in a photograph. At this point, I'd seen hundreds of orbs on photographs, and I'd seen blueish orbs in my photos, but I'd *never* seen a brilliant-blue orb like this one, and its timing was impeccable.

I shared this photo with the orb group that I had created on social media. My friend Amy commented, "Could it be a 'blue moon'?" What a great comment! Yes, it was a brilliantly blue orb—but it wasn't a moon. It was perfect in every way, and the blue orb will always be one of my favorite photos.

Orbs are incredible gifts in and of themselves, but like Robert's heart-shaped red rocks, their gifts stretch beyond themselves too. For years now I have searched through old family photos, collected others' photos, and taken new ones of my own, trying to connect the dots—literally and figuratively! Sometimes I stop and wonder, to what end? What would this work ever mean, to me or to anyone?

I made peace with myself by seeing the goodness in my doing *something*. I am researching, taking pictures, seeing new and different orbs and colorful streams of light on photos. I am talking about my experience at museums and book clubs just because I enjoy talking with others and hearing their stories. Not knowing where any of this will lead, or what any of this means, still, doing *something* is better than doing *nothing*.

If you are interested in orbs and taking photographs of them, don't ever worry about what other people will think or say about you. I know that's easy to say, but I encourage you to listen to me. Our message is important.

It simply may not be for some people, but that doesn't mean you should keep it from those who need it. You must honor your message because there are people who are watching and waiting and hoping to see something good in this world.

One of those beautiful nights at my friend Amy's creative retreat in Georgia, I sat on my balcony in the late evening, thinking about so many things. Our lives, our relationships, how we respond and interact with each other. How we can work together to achieve common goals, to create a peaceful existence for our future. The question on my mind that night was "How do we live with a steady peace of mind in this unstable world?" How, knowing that our lives can change with the blink of an eye?

Is it a mindset or is it a belief system?

I looked at the trees around the complex. Our trees are critical to our existence, even in the dark, I could see their beauty. Earlier in the day, I'd lain on one of the several hammocks stretched between the trees. The trees around Oconee Lake are so tall, when you're swinging in the hammock, their trunks look like they can reach the sky.

I was looking into the trees, and only one word was on my mind, so I said, "Help." That was all I could think of when I thought of this world. I took a picture of the tree that was directly in front of me.

In the photo, there is a glowing, ringed, peach-colored orb on that green tree. This is a first for me, seeing this particular color, which makes it unique. There will always be people who will say that this Georgia-peach orb is simply a reflection from my camera's lens, but I don't care. I know what was happening at the time I took the photo, and that's all I really need.

Visit:
www.SandyMayberry.com to see her full collection of orb photos, videos and books.

Please Like & Follow
ORBS: A Message of Love on Facebook to get the latest updates.

CPSIA information can be obtained
at www.ICGtesting.com
Printed in the USA
BVHW032059260720
584328BV00001B/60